The Early Days of Marlborough College: Or, Public School Life Between Forty and Fifty Years Ago. to Which Is Added a Glimpse of Old Haileybury; Patna During the Mutiny; a Sketch of the Natural History of the Riviera; And, Life in an Oxfordshire Village

Edward Dowdeswell Lockwood

THE "CASTLE" INN OF COACHING DAYS.

(Now part of Marlborough College.)

THE EARLY DAYS

OF

MARLBOROUGH COLLEGE;

OR

Public School Life between Forty and Fifty Years ago.

TO WHICH IS ADDED

A Glimpse of Old Haileybury;

Patna during the Mutiny;

A Sketch of the Natural History of the Riviera;

AND

Life in an Oxfordshire Village.

BY

EDWARD LOCKWOOD,

Indian Civil Service (Retired),

AUTHOR OF "THE NATURAL HISTORY OF MONGHYR."

ILLUSTRATED.

LONDON :

SIMPKIN, MARSHALL, HAMILTON, KENT & CO., LIMITED;

FARMER & SONS, KENSINGTON, W.

1893.

FARMER AND SONS,
PRINTERS,
295, EDGWARE ROAD, LONDON,
W.

PREFACE.

 OFTEN hear it said that no school turns out better scholars than Marlborough; and certainly I have no reason to doubt this fact, for even in my time it was by no means behind other schools in this respect. Indeed there is good reason to suppose that there is no better school all round, for after my time there appears to have been a thorough reform and cleansing of the Augean stable, effected, I imagine, chiefly by raising the terms, and obtaining sufficient raw material necessary for the manufacture of the sleek and happy schoolboy. In holding up a mirror of early days there, I am merely giving a brief account of the place as I knew it. I was unfortunate in going there in its tentative days, when cheapness was overdone, for after all other expenses had been paid, there could not have been much left over to provide efficient masters and sufficient food out of the £15 which my father paid each half-year for me, particularly as I find, on

reference to corn averages, that bread was then at least double the price it is now.

At the same time, should anyone invite me to give an apt illustration to the text That "Creation groaneth and travaileth until now," it would be that mathematics and dead languages—the most dry and uninteresting of all subjects, except to an elect few—form the chief items in the curriculum of our schools; and that the elect, who, as a matter of course, preside over the schools, understanding and delighting in these subjects, are apt to give short shrift and little commiseration to dull fellows like myself, who don't—or at least didn't at the age of eight—share their knowledge and enthusiasm.

Those who are not fully aware how much humbug—unconscious no doubt—there is, even amongst the best of men, may feel surprised that the great moralist, and generally reasonable Dr. Johnson, should always have expressed his approbation of enforcing instruction by means of the rod; and yet, not only do we find him beating his schoolmistress, but also bitterly complaining of his master. "He used," he said, "to beat us unmercifully, and did not distinguish between ignorance and negligence." If such things were done to the green tree, what must have been done to the dry? If the owner of such an intellect complains, how must the dunces have suffered? We also find Boswell and his patron laying their heads together to defend a ruffian—whose salary appears to have been only £20, and therefore plainly of the cheap and nasty type—who had been "somewhat severe" in the chastisement of his scholars. "This man," says the great moralist, " has maimed none of his boys ; they are all left with the exercise of their corporeal faculties. In our schools in England many boys have been maimed ; yet I never heard of an action against a schoolmaster on that account." But the subject is too horrible to continue, and it may be considered very presumptuous on my part in venturing to imply, *" Maxime ! si tu vis, cupio contendere tecum."*

The great classical scholar and writer of the next century also, so far as I can make out, ranges himself on the side of the rod. I don't remember that Macaulay's biographers mention that he was ever beaten at school ; if he was, it must have been for turning the tables on his teachers, and exasperating them by knowing too much. He seems to think that a boy even deserves a flogging for using the word θνητοι in the same sense to which the Right Honourable John Wilson Croker, (no mean Greek scholar) ascribed to it.

But when such authorities as these are for hammering boys, no wonder that dull children, on leaving home for school, incline to exclaim with me,

> " And turning from my nursery window, drew
> A long, long sigh, and wept a last adieu."

I have always felt sore when recalling my school-days, but now I have had my say in the following pages, I feel like Mr. Pickwick, after he had pitched into Dodson and Fogg in his lawyer's office ; and I am happy in raising my voice against the rascally trick some masters have, or at least had in my time, of scamping their work, and making their wretched pupils suffer in consequence,

On looking over my manuscript I find I have made several Latin quotations, and I fear I incur the risk of making myself supremely ridiculous in posing as a Latin scholar. Nothing however can be further from my intention, for no one can be more painfully aware than I am myself, how great my ignorance is, not only in Latin but in every other branch of knowledge. Perhaps I should act wisely in striking out all the Latin. But I trust it will not be considered offensive when I acknowledge I am merely gifted

"With just enough of learning to mis-quote,"

and have had to refer to the originals before venturing to send what I have written to the printer. Ever since I took up the Georgics for examination they have been running in my head, and as I have kept a large apiary for many years, I believe I have read the Bee-poem more frequently than any other book. But perhaps I had better not say anything more on the subject, for in trying to avoid one rock I may get wrecked upon another, and being accused of the pride which apes humility, find myself in the position of the old man and his donkey, who, do what he would, failed to satisfy his critics.

What a wonderful thing is memory! Although I am far too apt to forget, after five minutes have elapsed, who dealt last, and whether the Queen is out before putting down my Knave, events which occurred nearly fifty years ago so crowd my memory, that my chief fear in writing my manuscript has been that it will be too long, and illustrate the vice of prolixity, so current at the present time. I find also that I have not placed all my stories of school life in strict chronological order. They have recurred to my memory whilst working on my farm—whilst mingling with the universe by the brook-side and elsewhere—so I experienced difficulty in placing them exactly in their proper places without considerable loss of time and trouble. But although I should not have minded this, if absolutely necessary, I venture to think that changing about from one subject to another will render what I have written less tedious than otherwise it might have been.

Scraps of my text, here and there, have appeared in print before, and the whole of the last two chapters, "On the Riviera," were published in "*The Field*," so I have to express my thanks to the Editor for allowing me to reproduce them here.

The men who work on my farm and other residents of the village tell me they hope to read what I have written in the following pages. As comparatively few of them have extended their travels even so far as London, it appears to me that portions of my text which relates to mammoths, bull-fighting, and chasing painted ladies, might be misinterpreted without illustrations. I have accordingly introduced such pictures as I have found available, for their benefit; and I trust, if by chance the polite and learned remember having seen something similar before, that they will pass them over without unfavourable comment. Messrs. Blackwood, of Edinburgh, very kindly presented me with pictures of the mammoth and fish-lizard skeletons, and I am indebted to my niece, Miss Alice Lockwood, at the Rectory, for the portraits which appear on pages 36, 43, 71, 73.

EDWARD LOCKWOOD.

KINGHAM.

CONTENTS.

LIST OF ILLUSTRATIONS.

———

LIST OF ILLUSTRATIONS—*continued*.

THE EARLY DAYS OF MARLBOROUGH COLLEGE.

CHAPTER I.

LTHOUGH we cannot expect mankind to care much about remote posterity, I should feel grateful if the forefathers of the hamlet had taken the trouble to place on record the principal events which have occurred from time to time in our village here. Or better still, if each succeeding age had produced its Gilbert White, who would have told us not only who built the Rectory,* and the houses whose walls are four feet thick, but also how the village fared when the wolf's howl was re-echoed from the church tower, and eagles, cranes, and bitterns frequented the valley of the Evenlode.   We might also have learnt

* On a memorial marble in the Church, one Dowdeswell, an ancestor of mine who flourished during the reign of James II., is alluded to as *hospitii vicini fundator*.   According to "The Antiquary," the *hospitium* was a place for entertaining strangers, and this description would certainly apply to the Rectory since I have known it.

B

how the Saxons employed their time, and who was the king† that made this place his home, and how far his sovereign rule extended.

And going further back, we should like to read some record of those days, when the Georgics formed our farmers' *vade mecum*, and when the soldier, who came here for an evening stroll from the Roman Camp close by, talked Latin with a purer accent and greater ease, than even the college tutor who adorns our village now.

How eagerly we should listen to a diary kept by that still older race which worshipped at the Rollright Stones, perched on the summit of a neighbouring hill; for we should like to hear about their sacrifices, and whether our village supplied any of their victims; and where the Druids got their supply of mistletoe, as none grows in the neighbourhood now.

Of the ancient inhabitants of our village, so far back, it may be said :

> Their bones are dust,
> Their swords are rust,
> Their souls are with the saints—we trust.

But before them, there appears to have lived a race, whose weapons have defied the mouldering hand of time ; whose flint arrow-heads and axes are now ploughed up, fresh as the day when they left the cunning hand which made them ; to slay their fellow-men of course, and also to do battle with the Mammoths, whose fossil bones were found by cartloads, when the cutting which divides my farm into two portions, was dug out by the navvies who made our railroad.

Wandering further up the stream of time ; what an eager crowd of savants would assemble to hear a true and faithful history of that huge boulder, which gives the name of " Great Stone " to one of my fertile fields, and the time when many thousand feet of ice and snow covered our village site.

---

† In Doomsday book this village is called Canyngeham or King's home, and to the present day a residence here is usually accounted so delightful, that the inhabitants are supposed to feel despondent, when out of sight of the church tower. My old friend, Master Beauchamp, whose brief military career is mentioned in another chapter, went a step further, for as he leant on his shepherd's crook beneath the trees on the village green, he was wont to declare, that he would sooner be *hung at Kingham* than die a natural death elsewhere.

Many ciphers would be required to write down in round numbers, the years which have passed since the "Great Stone" was deposited in my field, but even then our village site was old; though the small group of stars which are shining through my window now, and by

THE MAMMOTH.
A former inhabitant of our village site.

which I have often guided my boat upon the Ganges, may have been visible on clear nights, and puzzled primeval man to count.

*Quæ septem dici, sex tamen esse solent.

* The story of a missing Pleiad, originated I believe from an optical delusion, caused by the peculiar position of the stars which form the group. Viewed together they appear seven. The star-gazer perhaps does not notice them again for some time, and then counting them he not unnaturally exclaims that one is missing, as he can only find six (Of course I do not allude to professional star-gazers or astronomers.)

But the blue lias, which crops up in another of my fields, carries our record back to a far remoter period, when our village site lay at the bottom of the sea, upon whose waves, according to astronomers, constellations, unknown to us, were shining, and giving light to the strange and monstrous forms of life, whose bones are occasionally turned out by modern workmen.

The lias is the most ancient evidence which our village has to show of days gone by ; but a thousand feet below us there probably lies a bed of coal, which although it may be somewhat nearer to my door, than the Depôt at our Junction, unfortunately is far more difficult to approach.

THE SKELETON OF A FISH LIZARD (25 *feet in length*).
An inhabitant of our village site in lias days.

Those whose education is comparatively advanced, whilst viewing the various strata our village can exhibit, will "strive to turn the key of time, in order to comprehend the vast, the awful truth of the eternity which has gone by;" but many generations of working men have dug our lias, without giving its age and history a moment's thought.   To them as yet, the magic word "Geology" is quite unknown, though some, perhaps, will say :—

"Where ignorance is bliss, 'tis folly to be wise."

But whilst we may deplore the absence of ancient books or manuscripts, relating to the history of our village, future inhabitants will have little cause to complain of us who live here now. We have our Gilbert White in my neighbour, Mr. Fowler,* the historian

* Fellow of Lincoln College, Oxford.

of birds; and Colonel Barrow, F.R.S., who lives opposite, with an instinct probably inherited from his father,* keeps a "Log," which has attained such gigantic size, that it weighs four hundred pounds, completely putting in the shade those burly† volumes, which Macaulay reviewed with the remark, "that the prolonged years of Hilpa and Shalum, who lived before the flood, are required to read them through."

My acquaintance with our village dates from a time when railroads in the neighbourhood were unknown, and when anyone who had been to London was considered a *bonâ fide* traveller—a man who had seen the world—an oracle.

Farmer Shirley was one of these, and as he stood leaning on his gate, clad in the leather heirloom-breeches of those days, he seemed never weary of relating to a gaping crowd, how on reaching the metropolis, thinking that the people, from their numbers, must be coming out of Church, he planted his back firmly against a wall waiting till they should all go by. According to his own account, he might have waited there for ever; had not some careless person dropped a five-pound note close by upon the pavement; He could hardly believe his eyes: tradition said the London streets were paved with gold, but here was "paper" for the trouble of picking up! He was about to pocket his lucky find, when a stage whisper reached his ears, "Halves countryman!" it seemed to say, and looking round, he found another pair of eyes had seen the note upon the ground. At first the farmer indignantly refused to share the spoil, but threatened pains and penalties caused him to hand over all the cash he had, some thirty shillings, to pacify the man, who, grumbling, went his way.

The heated controversy had made the farmer thirsty, so, turning into a neighbouring tavern, he called for a glass of beer, tendering of course the note in payment. But he was informed it had no

* Sir John Barrow, Bart.; for many years Secretary to the Admiralty, a great traveller and a voluminous writer; died 1848.

† It was not until I had written this sentence down, that I discovered I incur the risk of making persons with sensitive ears, "ashamed of their species."

commercial value, and he narrowly escaped detention as a forger; and almost worse than that, on looking round, he found his dog, to which he was much attached, was gone.   Then our worthy neighbour's brief visit to the metropolis ended; and turning his distorted visage homewards, he stepped bravely out to walk the seventy miles before him, begging food and water by the way.

Next day he reached his home; a wiser, if not a sadder, man; for any chagrin which still remained from his unlucky trip to London, was dispelled, when with astonishment—akin to that with which he viewed the note upon the ground—he saw his dog rush out joyously, to welcome his return.*

About that time, or say half-a-century ago, a scheme, which had been proposed to turn the old Castle Inn at Marlborough, into a College, which should give a liberal education, on very favourable terms, to the sons of clergy, met with the warm approval, not only of my father, who was the Rector here, but also of my brother and myself, who were to enjoy the advantages set forth.   The prospect held out before us, was painted in rosy hues.   Happiness, we were told, is the special heritage of schoolboys.   We should drink of the fountain of knowledge freely, and thus acquire power; and what perhaps was the most important item in our eyes, we should receive a piece of silver, all of which we might fairly call our own, as each succeeding Saturday came round.

Although, as yet, our English was imperfect, and we knew nothing of the language of ancient Greece and Rome, what did it matter! "Leave all that sort of thing to us," cried the interviewed preceptor, with an ominous flourish of his arm; "We will soon explain to these little chaps what *relativum cum antecedente concordat* means, and we will introduce them to those jolly rural vocalists, Mopsus and Silenus; to the fair Œnone, and the faithless Paris."

In the August following, on the 12th day—though on this point I

---

* About this time the late Lord Redesdale, the local magnate of those days, in a letter to my father, which I have seen, and is still extant I believe, at the Rectory, wrote, "I trust you will oppose, by every means in your power, this horrid railway, which will cut up many of our finest meadows." Notwithstanding this sage warning, my father did all he could to promote the railway.

am not quite sure—my father's carriage-and-pair was drawn up by the Rectory door; and by the time my brother and myself, aged nine and eight respectively, were hoisted up behind, no party, *en route* to the moors, contained a more happy and contented quartette than that carriage did. The Rector and his wife in front, thinking that their children would now "get on," and traverse the road to fortune; whilst we behind were full of hope and joy, longing for the Elysian fields at Marlborough College, in which we were so soon to revel. In the foreground of the picture stood our youthful postman, who had just arrived with letters, and on the Rectory steps our faithful *cordon bleu** appeared, with a basket of provisions to help us on our way. This good lady often told us, in after years, that she could not help feeling somewhat disappointed at our radiant faces, as she held our hands in hers, wishing us "good-bye," and as she had experienced the vanity of human wishes, she entertained grave doubts regarding the anticipated peace and joy, stored up for us in the new world we were going to explore.

The most fascinating theory of modern science tells us, that no scene on which the sun has shone is absolutely lost, as the reflection goes travelling on, with great velocity, for ever through the sky. That, given the proper distance and suitable optical instruments, or eyes, every scene which has occurred on earth may now be viewed. The forests, which formed our coal, in all their pristine beauty; the monsters which thronged the seas and air in lias days, unscared by man. So perhaps beings who inhabit planets, which move round stars of the second or third magnitude, may, as I write, be feasting their celestial eyes upon my form just entering Marlborough College.

However that may be; the scene of my introduction lay in the "wilderness and mount" attached to the College grounds, a damp and creepy-looking place, apparently laid out in days gone by, when buff-jerkins were about; and, judging from the prevalence of yews,

* These two persons are introduced as a tribute to the salubrity of our village. The former, Tom Phipps, is still our postman; and the latter, at the age of 92, is superintending the preparation of my dinner now.

when the English armed themselves as remote savages do now. The clergy, as might be expected, were in force, bringing in a stream of new arrivals, full of life and joyous mirth.

One group of lads was engaged in hunting frogs which abounded there, and great heaps of the slain were prominently exposed to view; whilst the captain of the crew, like Agamemnon, was chiding the backward, and encouraging the zealous ones to renewed exertions. Every hole and corner was carefully explored, and reptiles, which scenting danger, had crept into fastnesses under logs or stones, were remorselessly dragged out. The moat also, which bounded the wilderness on one side, was searched by an eager band, with sleeves turned back, in order to probe the overhanging banks, and draw out the slimy prey. Some were stripping nut-trees of their fruit, whilst others, more to show their prowess, than to illustrate Darwin's "Descent of Man," which had not then appeared, were climbing trees, and amid the branches, peeping down with gay grimaces on the passers-by.

The sports of children satisfy the child; but the parents soon grew weary of the scene, and thinking that their brood might be shipped off fairly now, retired to spend a quiet evening at the "Ailesbury Arms," which, doubtless, at that time was doing a roaring trade. Then I was left alone, and eager to give full play to my buoyant spirit, at once made overtures to gambol with a rough-looking sturdy lad, under whose wing I hoped to bask in safety, as he appeared a giant in my eyes. But he, resenting these advances, aimed a furious blow with a thick frog-slaying bludgeon at my head, which would have knocked out the scanty brains I possessed, and ended my schooldays for ever, had I not, with the agility of a puma, jumped aside and fled in terror. But, as I fled, an imprecation was wafted through the evening air, which sounded like, " O, damn the bugs*; I hate the bugs; I should love to slay them all."

This early lesson made a deep impression on my mind; it showed how true the Eastern proverb is—*admi ka Shaitan admi hai,* which

* This elegant *sobriquet* was applied to all the boys of the Lower School.

means to say, "that man's greatest enemy is man," or, in other words, that the proverb, "Hawks don't pick out hawks' eyes," cannot be applied to boys.

It is all very well for the poet to exclaim :—

> " How I love the festive boy
>   With his tripping dance of joy."

but the ordinary small schoolboy is not regarded with much favour by outside mortals bigger than himself. The old Hanuman monkeys of India, are said to kill the youthful males, whenever they can catch them; and I have little doubt the lads of the Lower School would soon have shared a similar fate, had they not been protected by the law. This opinion was subsequently confirmed by a poem, composed in Greek, by a forward boy of the Upper School, and which was shouted out amid uproarious mirth by all who were sufficiently advanced in learning. It was known as " The Doctor's war-song over the Lower School bugs," and although I knew very well its import, I could only catch the refrain, which sounded like—"*Zeus, Zeus, katakteine astrapo!*" Which seems to mean, that as the big fellows dare not polish us off themselves, an urgent appeal was made to Jupiter, to " do the needful," and exterminate us, bag and baggage, with his thunder-bolts.

Two lads who were present in the wilderness attracted my particular attention. Indeed, they formed the cynosure of all. One was the only boy in the school who possessed those fearful appendages to the human face, called whiskers, which in those days excited general admiration, and were supposed to make the wearer irresistible to the other sex. In my Liliputian eyes, he appeared tall as the tree which stands before my window now, but as I find its height is more than thirteen feet, he could hardly have been so tall as that. This lad, on referring to the College register, I find has long since been dead; but the other, a graceful lad, also of monstrous height, is now Ambassador at Washington. I never heard his name mentioned except in praise, so there seems no harm in his introduction here. Neither of these sons of Anak took any part in the revels going on, but I sidled up, hoping to hear them speak. I remember every word they said, their dress, their attitude, and how they moved their arms and legs. Their conversation, although intensely interesting to me at the time, and listened to with wrapt attention, need not be repeated here, except the last sentence, which, as it is recalled, seems ringing in my ears, " I say, Whiskers! do you know if they intend to give us any tea ?"

We had not as yet learnt each other's names, and all were known by any peculiarity which seemed to attract attention. One was " Paddy," because of his brogue, another was " Skinny," because he was very thin, whilst a third was " Plum-Pudding," because he was very fat. There were also " Bears," " Monkeys," " Sheep," and " Pigs," from some unlucky supposed resemblance to those animals.

At length the school-bell rang for tea; and the boys who were still at play in the "Wilderness," were ushered into a large room, which forms, I believe, the College library now, overlooking the bowling-green. But the sickening smell of tea, boiled in new tin cans, was quite enough for me. Henceforward I became a strict abstainer, and during the eight-and-a-half years I remained at school, I invariably quenched my thirst at the College pump; thereby acquiring dexterity in making my hand a channel of communication with my mouth, which I often found useful whilst travelling in India and elsewhere.

Nor did the beer, which subsequently was dealt out at dinner, in any way alter my predilection for the pump; not that I was fearful it might make me skittish, but I failed to appreciate its stale, flat look, which was far from tempting. Some of the boys, however, who passed as connoisseurs, declared that it was not fit to drink, and a complaint to this effect apparently was made to the Council of the School. At all events a Councillor came down, and appeared one day attended by due ceremony, in the Dining-hall. There he stood for some moments, whilst a hum of expectation filled the air. At length he rapped the table with the handle of a knife, and when perfect silence reigned, he demanded in stentorian tones, that, what he was pleased to denominate "College ale," should be furnished him forthwith.

On that a lackey who had been waiting for his cue outside, appeared, with a jug and glass upon a tray. What an exciting scene that was to us, as the Councillor held the glass, now filled with ale, carefully to the light, scanning it narrowly with one eye closed, to make quite sure no flies, or small deer of any kind were meandering there. Having satisfied himself thus far, he applied the potion to his nose; and then a smile lit up his countenance, such as we may suppose, stole over the face of the jolly god when first he heard an ode of Horace recited in his honour. Then he poured the glass of College ale down his throat, passed his hand over his waistcoat to make sure it was safe inside, and gazing blandly round amid the breathless silence of us all, he said "that during the entire course of an honourable career he had never tasted a more excellent glass of ale, than that which we had seen him now imbibe."

Of course no evidence was forthcoming, whether the ale, so highly praised, came from our cask, or whether the saying, * *In vino veritas*, could fairly be applied to him.

But I have wandered from the first entertainment at the College. Besides the tea, which I declined to drink, bread and butter was provided, but in such limited supply, that everyone was clamorous for more, and as there was no bell or other means of communication with the pantry, some hungry forward boy began to stamp his feet, an example which was quickly followed by us all. When this exercise had been carried on for some little time, a man, whom subsequently we knew as the College baker, put in an appearance, and greeted us with a sleepy smile of satisfaction, evidently at our appreciation of his wares. But when his paper cap and unkempt look, drew forth comments not wholly complimentary to himself, he stood eyeing us with a look which evidently he intended to be one of

---

* This means, that a man " in beer," will speak the truth. But I agree with Dr. Johnson, and should decline the acquaintance of a " fellow " who must be made drunk, before I could believe a word he says.

supreme contempt. At length, when his indignation would allow him to speak, he said " Wot! and haven't none of you never seen nobody before?" and having uttered this specimen of Marlborough grammar, he hurried off to report in a higher quarter, the anarchy which prevailed, whilst we shot forth another shaft which remained in our futile armoury.

My would-be assassin, from whom I could hardly remove my eyes, had ascertained that Rogers was the College butler's name; and he proposed, with the cordial approval of us all, that this high official should henceforth be summoned. The suggestion was accordingly carried out, in such shrill notes, that the only wonder seemed that the roof did not fall in, or the floor open and swallow up us all. No Rogers came, but in his place a master with a formidable cane appeared, and then we learnt our first lesson, that in future we must remain content with what the gods provided, and no more.

But whilst we had Scylla in the shape of hunger, on one hand, on the other, we subsequently found, was the more dangerous Charybdis—Mistake in gauging our appetites, and leaving food upon our plates.

" Waste not want not," is certainly a good motto to impress on those who are over-burdened with this world's goods; but at Marlborough College when I was there, opportunity of having anything to waste so seldom happened, that the aphorism might fairly have been regarded as a dead letter, or one which did not demand much notice. Those in authority however thought other- wise; and some time before we were dismissed from hall, a careful scrutiny of all our plates was made, in order to ascertain whether any young wolf among us was likely eventually to come to want, through wasteful conduct. .

The grating noise, made by the master's chair as he rose to make his rounds, or knout us in the school, is one of those familiar sounds, which I imagine has often been recalled by many an old Marlburian. I have fancied that I heard it in the lonely Indian jungles, and whilst lying on the banks of the sacred Ganges; and although night-mares seldom trouble me, that sound, or an examination paper, of which I cannot answer a single word, take the place of other terrors which troubled sleepers see.

There was a boy who was only seven when he arrived at school; he sat near me, and one day he whispered that he thought he could eat a house, meaning that he was very hungry. It was resurrection-day, on which a *réchauffé* was served up, surmounted by such a formidable crust, that a very limited portion would have made even sturdy Friar Tuck cry, "Hold, enough." But hunger had made my neighbour reckless, and he demanded a second slice; and then the dreaded Inspector stood before him. Perhaps terror checked his appetite; for, although he crammed the delicate morsels into his mouth, he found how true the saying is: *Naturam non expellas furca,* or, "You can't drive out nature with a fork." The master eyed his victim for some moments, which, though they may have been pleasant enough to him, were agony to the wretched boy; and at length, pulling out the well-known pocket book, he said, "Come to my desk when the school bell rings, and I will cane you."

How gladly the entire school would have hailed the sudden appearance of the Editor of "*Truth,*" or the Secretary of the Society for the Prevention of Cruelty to Children on the scene, to stay the reverend arm.

There was a tradition in the Lower School, that if any master raised his arm above his head whilst in the act of caning, he was liable to be fined a bottle of the best champagne. Whether this penalty was ever enforced in my case, I don't pretend to say, but, if it was, I certainly never received my share. Perhaps it was enforced in the "Common room," where, of course, the masters drank my health, hoping, at the same time, that the dose would be repeated soon.

When our first scanty meal at school was ended, as the days were long, we were all let loose into the large courtyard which is bounded by the iron railings, and there we had to make acquaintance

with our schoolfellows as best we could.   But as everyone wished
to curry favour with those older and bigger than himself, I, being
very small and young, met with scant courtesy from all.

Some large trees were standing near the covered playground then,
and under one of these Jefferies had his stall of cakes and tarts,
whilst under another tree, a woman whose name I can't remember,
had a stall of gooseberries, with which she did a roaring trade.
In fact, most of the money which the boys had brought from home
passed into the pockets of the stall-holders on that never-to-be-
forgotten day.   The gooseberry-vendor had every reason for satisfaction; for when she retired, having disposed of all her wares, she was
followed by a grateful crowd which cheered her to the echo, and
as she turned the corner leading to the town, the ovation which she
received as "*the cheap woman,*" must still have been ringing in her
ears.

At sunset Sergeant Bompas rang the school-bell suspended by
his lodge; the bell whose summons for many years I attended to so
well, that I never once was late.   Again we were ushered into the
room where we had enjoyed our so-called tea.   The strictest silence
was enforced, whilst I, overawed, felt like a mouse under a lion's
paw, and found the quiet which reigned around, a very painful
contrast to the unlimited amount of chatter in which I was wont to
indulge when I occupied my nursery at home.

At half-past eight the school-bell rang again, and then I was
introduced to an attic of the Old Castle Inn, overlooking the
bowling-green, which I shared with twenty other boys.   "Rules and
Regulations" were posted up, which, among other things enforced
silence, which was very irksome, for even rooks and starlings are
allowed to chatter when they go to roost.

A captain was placed over us, and as he was a new broom he
naturally desired to show his zeal, and not finding anyone inclined
to break the rules, he fixed on me, probably because I seemed least
likely to defend myself, and sent up my name to the head master
next day for talking, although I had hardly dared to breathe, much

less to speak.   But as time went on, this silence rule was not enforced, though talking seldom lasted long, for soon all the dormitories throughout the school were hushed in slumber.

The attic where we slept had probably, in its old inn days, sheltered many a weary traveller, who gladly would have changed places with either of the twenty urchins herded together there with me.   But the first few hours' experience of school-life caused me to lie down upon my iron bed—the first night which fell on Marlborough College—in far from an enviable state of mind.

CHAPTER II.

Y father came next day to see how we had passed the night, and I, with many tears begged him to take me home. But this was not to be, so we went for consolation to the bureau, where a deposit for our expected weekly money, was by appointment to be made. Here we found an illustration of the vanity of human wishes, for the official in charge appeared aghast at the liberal or rather prodigal spirit, which had suggested silver, and he declared, that with a liberal *cuisine* such as we enjoyed, threepence per week would meet all our possible requirements not provided by the school.

Half-a-sovereign in gold was consequently laid down upon the desk, in payment for my brother and myself, until the Christmas holidays came round, and this amount was truly said to be more than most boys in England, and elsewhere, ever get or hope for.

I am sure in our village here, the children cannot get so much, judging from the persistent way in which they come singing Christmas carols. Careless alike of wind and cold, they come, weeks before the customary time, and appear happy and contented if a dozen of them get a bronze coin to divide. But, perhaps, the fun of hearing their own voices, and making a noise, which they know no one appreciates but themselves, like the lemon which Jack Wilks handed to Dr. Johnson, gives a zest to the discomforts they undergo in the pursuit of gain.

It is an ill wind which blows no one any good, and, so tradition ran, the handsomely bound prizes, which were awarded to better boys than I, were paid for, on the principle of robbing Peter to pay Paul, from the fines imposed on the weaker brethren. And when the long-looked-for Saturday came round, and after much hustling and struggling with a crowd of other urchins, I reached the master who distributed the coin, demanding my loaves and fishes, he only gave me a stony stare, and curtly said, I might apply again on that day month, for I had been fined a shilling for swarming up a tree.

I attempted to prove an alibi in vain. But at length I demonstrated to the detective who sent in my name, that it was a case of mistaken identity. He declined, however, to stultify himself, and get back my coppers. "It was my own fault," he said, "I should not be so like the other boy." Young as I was in the ways of the world, I certainly considered this proceeding hardly fair, particularly as the numbers which were marked on our clothes formed an easy clue to identification, and as a rule, those who required information would not hesitate to grab our caps, and slyly peep inside, much to our mortification, and the entertainment of strangers passing by.

These numbers formed a never failing source of great delight to forward maidens in the town, for in the gloaming, when we were all locked up, they would appear in galaxies in front of the railings by the broad Bath road, where, attracting our attention by various antics and grimaces, they would point the finger archly, and declare that although they might not know our names, they were well acquainted with our numbers; amid the ecstatic laughter of the bystanders.

My weekly allowance was so often confiscated for some offence, real or pretended, that it was hardly worth a struggle presenting myself at the distributing chamber as each succeeding

c

Saturday came round, and consequently, like most of the other boys, I was very short of cash, which was sadly needed to buy food, especially during Lent, when we were well-nigh famished.

I remember with much gratitude all the money given me by outsiders, and on counting it up, I find it amounts to £1 12s. 6d., during the eight-and-a-half years I remained at school.

The post-office officials were not so clever at detecting coin in letters then as they are now, and it was a red letter day when we found a coin, however small, inside an envelope sent by some never-to-be-forgotten friend. Whenever I detected coin, which of course was very seldom, I retired where I could open the envelope unobserved, for unless the money was a good round sum, it was very likely viewed with scorn by my companions, particularly by those who never got anything at all.

A lad who sat next me, opening an envelope one day, incautiously allowed a sixpence to fall out upon the table: and the small amount caused considerable laughter, mingled with sarcastic comments, very mortifying for the small recipient to hear. But he was equal to the occasion,—pretending to read the letter through, he suddenly called out, "Aha! its all right! you fellows have no need to laugh, because I find, this piece of silver is merely a pioneer, in order to ascertain whether a piece of gold, which is to follow, can travel safely without detection."

My grandmother, who lived at the house with a bay window in Portland Place, occasionally sent me presents, but, as she was told that I fared "sumptuously as a king" at school, these generally took the shape of books, and on one memorable occasion she sent me "Hewitson's Eggs of British Birds," which first appeared about that time. Although this work cost seven guineas I believe, money was seldom better spent, its contents being much more suited to my taste or mental calibre than grammar, and it is on my bookshelf now.

As the old lady I have mentioned hailed from Ireland, she was possessed of considerable native humour, and one day I received

"But there, no Bernard dog, no convent bell,
Naught but the wolf to howl their parting knell.

Naught but th' Aurora, bursting through the gloom,
A torch to light them to their icy tomb."

From a Marlborough Prize Poem.

C2

from her a box of tablets, made with soap, to resemble gaily coloured eggs. But these I did not care about, as the school was liberal in the washing line. I was not satisfied however until I had cut one open and tasted it, when finding further examination useless, I presented box and all to the detective who had mistaken my identity, hoping he would remember me another time.

Once I received a small hamper from Algiers, and on opening it I found it contained, to my great delight, eggs, real eggs this time, of the Roller, Bee-eater, and Barbary-partridge, all rare "British birds." I did not meet the donor until many years had passed, and then I told him how much pleasure he had given me ; I said I had marked my calendar with a red letter on that day ; I had thought of him in Palestine, when I found a colony of Bee-eaters building in a sand bank, and so on, until he laughingly replied, that I reminded him of the Yankee proverb, " Cast thy bread upon the waters, and it shall return to thee, *as buttered toast*, after many days."

Several officers of the Franklin expedition dined at my grand-mother's house shortly before they set out on their disastrous arctic voyage, and Captain Fitz-James, who had taken a liking to me, begged my people to let me accompany the expedition. Perhaps my alleged propensity for climbing trees was considered good training for keeping a sharp look-out from the mast-head. But destiny had decreed that I should earn my bread within the tropics, and so the proposal to turn me into a sailor came to nothing.

The Franklin expedition subsequently formed the subject of a prize poem at Marlborough College, and considering the narrow escape I had, I took much interest in it, and something resembling a cold shudder came over me when the poet read out the lines, which I have some reason to remember, and which I have always thought are very good.

> " But there, no Bernard dog, no convent bell,
> Naught but the wolf to howl their parting knell,
> Naught but th' Aurora, bursting through the gloom,
> A torch to light them to their icy tomb."

Although I remember with gratitude, all the kind donations which I received at school, one memorable half-crown proved of very little use to me. A relation came posting through the town one day, and remembering I was there, sent for me, and handed me the coin I have mentioned, at that part of the road opposite to a pastry warehouse much frequented by the school; and when the carriage rolled away I naturally strolled into the shop, to have a look round, with the satisfaction of possessing power to purchase anything tempting which I saw.

Unfortunately, I happened to arrive just as the stock of tarts, which had been exposed for sale for many days, was being removed to make room for fresher wares; and the assistant in charge, who had spied the interview which I had been holding near the carriage, guessing that I was a capitalist, declared that I should make a splendid bargain if I accepted all his damaged stock, in exchange for the coin in my pocket. Contrary to my better judgment, I took the bait, for several boys had come in, and were nudging me, and having concluded the bargain, I gathered up my tarts, and hotly pursued by a swarm of other boys, I hastened to the school, where I shovelled my purchase into the desk which had been allotted for my use.

The desk had no sort of fastening, and my only hope appeared to be in taking up a position on top of the desk, and defending my property as best I could.

What chance had a lad of eight, weighing about four stone, of keeping back a legion of other boys all as hungry as himself? They began the attack certainly with fair words, and politely demanded that I should furnish them with a tart apiece, but finding me deaf to their entreaties, they changed their tactics altogether, and declared I was a little sneak for not sharing their socialistic views. Then, what I thought a bright idea, occurred, I would bribe the biggest boy to help me, and keep the others back. But when I descended from my perch, and opening the desk, displayed the tempting goods inside, the surging crowd no longer could be restrained, for casting all decorum to the winds, they made a sudden rush, which sent me flying over and over, till at last I landed on my back upon the floor. And by the time I had regained my legs every tart was gone.

If any of those robbers are living now, and have those tarts upon their conscience, perhaps they will be glad to hear that I give them absolution; for, on mature reflection, I admit that our life at school was one continued struggle for existence, with a survival of the fittest. Probably their consciences give them very little trouble; for many years after, whilst shooting in the Himalayas, I suddenly appeared before one of those very knaves of tarts sitting quite unconcernedly beneath a Tamarind tree, and after mutual recognition, the incident I have mentioned was recalled; but so far from producing expressions of sorrow or regret, it caused such peals of laughter, in which I was fain to join, that all the game in the vicinity was scared away, and the woods, which subsequently we beat together, were drawn blank.

This knave and I joined camps, and after dinner, before a roaring fire of logs outside, old Marlborough stories vexed the drowsy ear of night to such a scandalous extent, that our Jemadar at last, with folded supplicating hands, heading a deputation, said, "*Huzoor! Iskool kì kahàni na bolìye, kiswaste tamam ràt banda log ko nind nahin ata,*" which, after compliments, means that our Marlborough stories kept the entire camp awake.

This tart incident showed very clearly that, notwithstanding my companions' studies in Latin grammar, they had still very hazy ideas regarding the correct translation of *meum* and *tuum;* so that any property I had, or might hereafter acquire, would never be safe unless properly secured under lock and key.

An order had lately been promulgated to the effect that any lad who wanted a "playbox" could have one, with the consent of his people at home, given by letter to the writing and ciphering master. So I scrawled a letter home, evidently under the impression that because I knew the writing master's name myself, everybody else, of course, must know it too. A short time after, I heard what to me was really a dreadful sound. Like Alexander Selkirk, I gave a start when anyone called my name out loud. In answer to the summons, I went to the writing master, who seemed to sit uneasy in his chair, and on his desk lay an open letter, which I recognised at once. He said, but not unkindly, that a ridiculous mistake had taken place, for my mamma had mistaken him for the carpenter, and ordered him to make a box for me. I might perhaps have said that anyone who did not know him would proclaim himself unknown; but I had learnt the golden rule of silence, and was dismissed with the remark that the necessary order should be given, *but in the proper quarter.*

So far so good, I thought; but when the playbox came, and was duly deposited in the covered-playground, I had no property whatever to put in it. I had not long to wait, however. It was autumn time, and the air was redolent with apples—a scent agreeable to boys as toasted cheese is to a half-starved mouse. I sniffed the tainted gale; and presently saw a man struggling behind a barrow which contained a hamper of unusual size, on which there fluttered on the breeze a label bearing the name of a little boy I knew. I hastened to him, told him the joyful news, and soon my newly acquired key was drawn from my pocket and transferred to the depths of his. Then I strolled away, and ran over in my mind the apples which I liked the best.

Such were my thoughts when, with a wild hurrah, I saw my friend shot out of the parcel-room, followed by his hamper, supported by as many stalwart lads as could find a place around it, whilst a cry of " Apples ! apples ! " re-echoed from the walls of the quondam inn, and was passed from mouth to mouth, until pretty well the whole school took up the scent and had assembled there.

At length the covered playground was reached, and then the surging mass of boys was so great around my box, that little hope remained that anything destructible could hold together. It was quite impossible to get near; but I heard my property cracking from afar, and in less time than it takes me to record the fact, every apple had disappeared, and my box was smashed to atoms.

My friend, when he could extricate himself, was a truly piteous sight. Newly-made cider poured down his hair and face from the over-ripe fruit crushed up against him; first, in his endeavour to protect his property and mine, and then in his frantic efforts to escape. He very generously offered to recompense me for my loss—at some future time. But I made no claim, particularly as he had no assets of any kind; and, after all, it was no great loss to me, for I don't remember that I ever had any property which I could have put in my playbox had it remained intact.

Whilst these scenes of rapine were being enacted out of doors, there was not much inside the school which seemed likely to fulfil the forecast which had been made at home, that my school days would be full of joy. I was placed in the lowest class, and left to learn the Latin grammar by myself; for no one ever took the slightest trouble to teach me anything.

My master eyed me askance when I went up to class, and murmured that a certain pricking, or itching in his thumbs, led him to suppose that he must use his cane. A forecast which I found was much more likely to come true than those which had been made at home. The lessons appeared to him so easy, that he failed to comprehend why I should find any difficulty at all, and so, obeying the aphorism of Solomon, if I declined learning the three concords or agreements in Latin, he would endeavour to beat them into me with his cane.

The knoutings which I received from my master's reverend arm, turned my back all the colours of the rainbow; and when I screamed from the fearful torture they produced, the head-master would send a prefect down to say, that if I made such a horrid noise, he also would have a go-in at me, when my master had done his worst.

Occasionally two masters would be caning at the same time, with the rhythm of blacksmiths hammering on an anvil.

*Illi inter sese magna vi brachia tollunt
In numerum.**

A village schoolmaster now-a-days, I am glad to say, would get a
month at the treadmill, with a sinister caution as to his future
behaviour, if he beat a boy as I was beaten at school, and when,
on my arrival home, I was undressed and put to bed by my tender-
hearted nurse, she viewed my back with the utmost horror and
indignation. But she was told that as the punishment had been
administered by reverend men *called to the ministry*, I must have
deserved every blow I got.

I don't remember however that she was ever told *who* had called
them, and I was far too young, and inexperienced to demand an
enquiry with even the faintest scintilla of success.

In after years, when I looked up the Latin grammar, to which in
the meanwhile, some sensible and humane scholar had added an
English translation, it seemed easy enough, and I wondered why I
ever found any difficulty in understanding it, until I caught an
ordinary boy of eight years old, and began teaching him: then the
mystery was solved at once.

When I was still a little chap, and when there was but one school-
room for us all, some fifth form boys became stage-struck, and much
to my delight, gave a small theatrical performance, which I saw very
well by standing on a desk.

The play was of a nature very agreeable to boys, and was called,
I think, "Storming the Robbers' Den." Although no properties were
forthcoming, the scene was supposed to lie at a castle, surrounded
by a gloomy forest, which the band of robbers looked on as their
own. Suddenly a scout gave notice, that an attacking party had
arrived close by, and hardly were the words out of his mouth, than
a number of assailants appeared upon the scene, and a desperate
hand to hand encounter took place at once. Each party was armed

* "With lifted arms they order every blow,
    And chime their sounding hammers in a row."
                                    Dryden's Translation.

with weapons which looked like billiard cues, but as they were made of paper, what appeared tremendous blows could be inflicted without much damage being done. The fight went on so long as the paper held together, and then amid vociferous cheering, the so-called play was over.

But whatever it may be called, it was so decided a success that it was determined to put upon the stage something more elaborate and better. Tickets, price fourpence each, were accordingly issued to cover expenses, and a fearful Tragedy, aided by three clowns, was forthwith set in motion, and in due time placed upon the stage.

The spectators were disappointed, for the play was very dull. Even the three clowns, to whom we looked for fun, were melancholy exasperating fellows, who imbibing from the atmosphere around, the curious notion that rudeness is synonymous with wit, confined themselves chiefly to grimacing, and springing, monkey-fashion, at the gas lamps overhead. Occasionally they would hurl opprobrious epithets, of the *equi te esse feri similem dico** order at each other's heads, or long false ears, a style of wit at which only old Horace, or the friends of Peter Magnus, could possibly have smiled.

The author of the play, whoever he may have been, like Churchill, was "a barren rascal,"† for even the most lively imagination could not discover what it was all about. The Hero, chosen for his supposed *distingué* air, strutted about the stage, clad in a velvet suit, and slouched hat, surmounted with an ostrich feather, which no doubt absorbed most of our entrance money, and as he turned his back upon us nearly all the time, we could only catch here and there a word he said. At length he threw upon a table a dagger and a rope, but whether these were to polish off himself or someone else was left involved in doubt and mystery.

The Heroine was an effeminate-looking lad, clad in the fearful petticoats of those days, and to her belonged the credit of raising a solitary laugh, for treading on a paper rose, she picked it up, and

---

* Allow me to tell you, Sir, that I regard you as little better than a mad jackass.
† I have only the authority of Dr. Johnson for supposing that Churchill was "a barren rascal."

with a grimace, which the clowns would have done well to imitate, exclaimed, " Pretty flower, have I hurt you ? I will place you in my bosom to make amends !"

One master alone was present, but he soon nodded in his chair, and slumbered to the end, when he was unpleasantly aroused by the chorus of a song, to the tune of " John Peel," which was supposed to cast a reflection of his face, " when he called up his boys in the morning."

As the play fell so very flat, we heard no more of theatricals during the time I remained at school.

CHAPTER III.

ALTHOUGH among examples in the Latin grammar, which caused so much tribulation and so many tears in school, we find

O formose puer, nimium ne crede colori, *

no one could fail to notice, that the good looking, or rather pretty lads, were not so roughly treated as those less favoured by dame nature.

Mimicry in insects, is said to be a cause of protection against danger, and so Alexis or Hylas, who might easily be mistaken for Psyche, escaped the hard words and blows so freely showered on their plainer brethren.

"Old Chang" who occupied the next bed to mine, was a good-natured flat-nosed fellow with almond eyes. In China, amongst the heathen there, he might perhaps have passed as quite a beauty, but here he came in for more than his fair share of invective and execration. Had Chang been offered any choice, he would gladly have given his fellow students a wide berth, and by staying away from school, never have allowed his homely features to annoy them. but unfortunately he was helpless in the matter. The wind, according to a celebrated author, is tempered to the shorn lamb,

* Don't trust too much to your beauty, pretty boy.

though I never saw or even heard of a lamb deprived of its fleece myself,† and Chang, so long as the repugnance shown towards him was confined to words, sheered off, like Captain Cuttle, whenever danger threatened, and habit having acquired the phase of second nature, abuse which defiled its authors, although perhaps they did not think so, made no more impression on Old Chang than rain on the backs of water fowl.

We were enjoying some bread and cheese and radishes together, during the preparation hour one evening, just before retiring to rest, and as my friend was cramming these delicacies into his capacious mouth, the presiding master "twigged" him, and making a few rapid strides in our direction, and using his extended finger as a lance in rest, he assuredly would have transfixed one of Chang's almond eyes, had not that youth, who was always on the look out for thrusts, or blows, or kicks, ducked his head, and caused the master to fall over him.

> "Speak gently, for 'tis better far
>   To rule by love than fear,"

is good advice, but seldom followed at the school when I was there, and so soon as the master could recover himself from his undignified position, he roared out, as he prodded Chang in what we called the wind, "Great, coarse, gluttonous fellow! Go and stand out against the wall, and write me out one hundred lines of Ovid." Poor Chang had no kind friend to stand up for him in defence of his supposed personal defects, and in this he was not so fortunate as an ape once interviewed by me.

During my early years in India, I passed much of my time in company with Edward Blythe, who was then the accomplished curator of the museum at Calcutta. I was never weary of hearing him talk about beasts, or birds, or fishes, and occasionally I would

---

† My shepherd has since told me, that although lamb's wool, on account of its short staple, is of little value, dishonest farmers, when wool was worth half-a-crown per pound, instead of ninepence, as it is now, would shear forward lambs, and put the wool inside the ewe's fleece, to increase the weight. He has also known farmers send boys to pick wool off the hedges, where it had been torn by brambles, from the sheep.

accompany him to the native market, where we might find perhaps some rare bird, or curious fish, exposed for sale. One day we interviewed an orang-outang, possessed by a wealthy native, and I began in my usual reckless way, to make comments, far from favourable to the brute. Blythe heard me with impatience, for so far as I could learn, he thought every created thing fitted the situation it was called upon to occupy, and was beautiful in its way. "Come! come!" he said, "let us have no more of this, or I shall be compelled to tell you what that handsome ape is thinking now of you." And eyeing me askance, he muttered something which sounded like, "Those who live in glass houses should be careful how they fling mud or stones about."

"The Origin of Species" had lately been published, and I read with interest the correspondence which passed between Blythe and Darwin. One of the letters declared that the only critique on the Evolution theory, which demanded special notice, was one written by a friend of mine, a youthful member of the Geological Survey, and Darwin naïvely added, "My critic is a clever fellow;" as indeed he was.

Much as I appreciate the society of savants, it has very seldom been my good fortune to enjoy it; and the smattering of knowledge which I possess, certainly affords ample reason for learned men to give me what sailors call, plenty of sea-room.

The second time I was *en route* to India, on arriving at Marseilles, I ran down to the cabin of the steamer which was to take me to Alexandria, and put my card upon a plate in the saloon, as is the custom when anyone wishes to secure a place at dinner. The same evening, when all the passengers had assembled, I found myself seated next to an intelligent-looking gentleman, who listened good-humouredly whilst I talked on Natural History, and when the dinner ended, I generously declared that, as we should have plenty of spare time upon our hands during the coming week, I would put my neighbour into the way of knowing something about the classification of birds and other animals, and, if he liked, I would even go further,

and tell him about the strange forms of life which existed when the
world was young.

Afterwards, when I went on deck, I was talking to the captain,
and I told him how generous I had been. " By the bye," I said,
" who is that gentleman standing over there, abaft the binnacle?
He sits next to me at dinner."

THE CHAPEL, MARLBOROUGH COLLEGE.

(From a Photo by Seeley, Richmond Hill.)

" That gentleman," replied the captain, " is Pro—fessor Owen.
He is going to join the Prince of Wales in Egypt."

But although it can hardly be said that the shepherds who
presided over the flock at school, " allured us to brighter worlds and
led the way," they were determined that we should receive ample

religious instruction, such as it was. We were all driven, much against our will, fifteen times a week to Chapel, where the service was rendered far less irksome than it otherwise would have been, by the singing; for sufficient qualified voices were found among the host at school to form a choir, which, had I not known the boys, and watched their distorted faces whilst they sang, I might have imagined came down direct from heaven.

The choir also treated us to a concert of secular music and songs at the end of the half-year, when the excitement culminated with *Dulce Domum,* in which the lads of the whole school joined, of course at the summit of their voices. The great point aimed at was to make the final syllable of *resonemus* sound like a pistol, or rather, a cannon shot; and Old Chang, who sat next to me, would put his head almost between his knees, and when every echo of the chorus had died away, and all were inhaling as much air as possible to commence another verse, he would wildly scream out " *mus,*" as though his life depended on his arriving just in time to be too late, and had adopted *sero sed serio** for his motto. It had a very comical effect, and made everybody laugh. I wonder if this conceit has been executed at the Concerts since my time; or has the march of intellect made the boys consider themselves "a cut above it" now?

Naturally I longed to join this quasi-celestial choir, particularly as certain advantages were appended to it, and as I had often given " The ivy green," with much applause at home, I fancied I could sing. Accordingly I presented myself one day before the reverend man who presided at the choir, and in faltering tones informed him what I wanted. But a single glance at my face appeared enough for him to form an index to my throat. He did not tell me that my services were not required, in such courteous terms as—

> " Fusbos, give place !
> You know you hav'n't got a singing face."

* Late, but in earnest.

D

all he said, as he told me to go about my business, was—" I'll
be bound to say you have no more voice than a pig."

The rustics in the neighbourhood had a fixed idea that our sole
object in coming to school was to acquire manners. But if they
had any cause to complain about our want of courtesy, they would
not have expected much had they seen the example set us by our
betters. If dispensing civility were a luxury which can only be
indulged in by the rich, there would have been some excuse for the
rudeness we received at school; but considering that it costs nothing,
it might be surprising that we got so little, until we look outside the
iron railings, and see how prone mankind in general is to bully
those who cannot retaliate.

Sweeps, who in the great seminary outside, may be said to have
taken their places in the Lower School, tell me that the world, at
least the well-dressed portion of it, fear their resentment far too
much to be otherwise than polite and courteous whilst addressing
them. But tramps, without a home or friends, have often told me
they come in for much more than their proper share of rudeness,
though as a rule they say it does not affect them much. They get
so accustomed to it.

The " wilderness," where I was introduced to school, was soon
put out of bounds, but we could gaze into its dark recesses through
the railings which shut us out, and the tradition ran throughout the
Lower School, that fearful scenes were nightly enacted there, within
its gloomy caves and grottos.

Who were the actors on this dreadful stage? Where did they
hail from? Or why they should choose such a damp unpleasant
place, close to a school containing a host of boys? were questions
never asked or thought of. But one lad, who lingered near the
railings after the evening school bell rang, had heard distinctly, so
he said, most awful groans, as though the Thugs of India had taken
up their quarters, and were strangling a victim there. Another had
seen a mysterious light flitting to and fro among the trees, and
watched it until a piercing shriek sent him flying into the lighted

school.   Whilst a third was fully prepared "to take his dying oath,"
an expletive in frequent use at school, that he had heard somewhere
in that direction, an old woman's voice, exclaiming in heart-rending
tones, "Murder! murder! I'm lost! I'm lost!—For ever!" So
firmly did I believe these tales, that I retailed them to anyone who
would listen, when I arrived at home, and finding they were received
with suspicion accompanied by laughter, I became indignant, and
begged my people to write direct to Sergeant Bompas, and ask point-
blank whether I spoke the truth or not.

In recalling the early days of Marlborough College, the face and
form of Sergeant Bompas is pleasantly, if not affectionately remembered.   It was generally believed that he had fought at Waterloo,
and that the great victory was mainly due to him; but however that
may be, a deep dimple in his chin was pointed out as the scar of a
wound inflicted by the bayonet of a Frenchman, whose head Bompas
subsequently struck off.

I used to keep by the Sergeant's side whenever I saw him in the
playground; and with such a protector, I did not fear to walk about
the place, even at night when the mohawks were about, sweeping
the ground with a long rope, as sailors sweep for a lost anchor, and
of course upsetting us when the rope came in contact with our legs.
It was a very dangerous amusement, but I don't remember that it
lasted very long.

The story of Bompas having discomfited the French does not
appear to have been confined within the College grounds.   For
one day a tramp "in beer" appeared, and proclaiming himself in
unmistakable Irish accents to be a Frenchman, said that he had
come for the express purpose of avenging Waterloo, by challenging
Bompas to a single combat with his fists.   The Sergeant, who
probably had seen enough of fighting, and wished to end his days
in peace, instead of accepting the challenge, slipped off to the town
to fetch the Beadle, whilst the tramp was for the present left master
of the field, or rather, of the high-road, whilst the whole school
witnessed his triumph, shown in sparring at imaginary foes, capering

D2

about the place, and declaring he would fight the whole lot of us all put together, single handed.

I doubt whether Wellington, on that memorable day in June, looked more anxiously in the direction whence Blucher was expected to appear, than we did to the corner of the road leading to the town. How slowly each minute seemed to pass. But at length a shrill cry went up in exultation, "The Beadle! the Beadle!" and if ever a scene was mentally photographed on mortal brain, that one was fixed on mine. A gentle breeze was blowing at the time, and the appearance of the Beadle in cocked hat, blue coat, red plush breeches, white stockings, and pumps, the flowing garments swelling out, and floating in the gale behind, gave, in the distance, an appearance of a gaily decorated ship in full sail.

THE BEADLE.

The old man's hair was long, and white as snow, and he carried in his hand the staff of office, which ever and anon he brandished defiantly in the air above his head, whilst, in accents trembling from age, but certainly not from fear, glancing upwards to the high ground where we stood, in answer to our ringing cheers, he said, " I'm not afraid of him;" and then, shaking his head, he repeated the same encouraging words.

The entire unwashed population of Marlborough town followed in the old man's wake, whilst we now held our breath in expectation, and wondered how it all would end. It was, indeed, an impressive scene, and one well calculated to strike terror in the pseudo-Frenchman's heart, for after giving the Beadle one long drunken stare, he turned and fled down the Bath road, followed by such a scream of derisive jeers and laughter as never was heard near Marlborough town before.

The Beadle, after making a succession of bows with great dignity, then withdrew, amid great cheering from us all, so long as he and his tag-rag and bob-tail train remained in sight.

When all was over, Sergeant Bompas, somewhat crestfallen, reappeared upon the scene; and then a rumour flew from mouth to mouth that the tramp would certainly reappear, and, under cover of the night, murder Bompas while he slept. Personally, I feared that such a tragedy would occur, and I could not rest until I had the assurance of the Sergeant that, armed to the teeth, he intended to sit up all night, and be upon his guard.

But although, much to my relief, poor old Bompas survived that night, he did not long remain as my protector at the school. He was not quite up to the required standard as a detective, and he had a soul above the petty tyranny expected of him. He also closed his eyes to many youthful escapades, such as climbing trees, and going out of bounds. When the half-year ended, he would go into the town and buy cigars and medicine-bottles full of rum, which, we had heard, would keep us warm during the terrible cold journey home by coach.

I and another boy—but that must have been later on—subscribed from our journey-money, and got some of these supposed caloric generators, but as I did not relish either, my companion took my share, and got so drunk that he was obliged to be left behind. The meerschaum pipe which I had bought, however, was in my pocket on my arrival home. Our butler found it when he took down my clothes to brush, and it was the first thing which met my father's eyes on the dining-room table, when he came down to breakfast next morning. I was rather taken aback when I heard what had occurred, for in my joy at getting home, I had forgotten all about the pipe.   My father, wisely viewing the matter merely as a joke, made no unpleasant comments; whilst I, glad to get rid of the article altogether, presented it to my friend the postman, who tells me he has it now.

It must not be supposed however that I learnt absolutely nothing at school, for I learnt some useful lessons, which, although not directly set down in the curriculum of the school, were taught in a far more summary manner than I should have acquired them at home, and amongst these was the general truth of the saying—

> " O, what a tangled web we weave,
>   When first we study to deceive!"

One day there occurred to me what seemed a very bright and original idea.   Possibly I might escape many of the evils to which I was exposed at school, by placing myself on the sick list; and thinking such a ruse was one for which I might eventually take out a patent, I revealed it to my brother, who thought it so very ingenious that we determined to put it forthwith into execution.

Accordingly, assuming a sad and dejected air, we presented ourselves at the surgery and rang the bell, the sound of which frightened us not a little, as now there appeared no retreat, even had we wished it.

Presently a charwoman appeared and asked us what we wanted; to which we replied that we desired to see the doctor, as neither of us was feeling very well.   Thereon the good lady, who probably had picked up some knowledge of medicine, and its collateral incidents, gave us so very little encouragement, that, had we been wise, we should have bolted back to school.   But in our innocence, we sat down on a bench until the doctor should appear.

Dr. Gardiner was a very worthy man, and kind withal, for he always began a consultation with, "And what's the matter with you, dear boy?"   Report ran, that he had fought side by side with Bompas at Waterloo, and had horses killed under him on that eventful day.   But on our eventful day, as there was a clean

MARLBOROUGH COLLEGE, OVERLOOKING THE BOWLING-GREEN.

The old Attic mentioned is shown here.

bill of health, unfortunately for us, he deputed an assistant of the Jack Hopkins stamp to attend the surgery, and this youth presently came striding in, and greeted us with such a loud "Hulloa!" that had we been suffering from some nervous disease, it would have done us quite as much good as an electric shock. After running his eye over us for some moments, he curtly demanded from my companion information as to what ailed him, and receiving the answer, which we had previously agreed upon, "A headache and a pain in my side," he burst out laughing, and turning to me, said he would go bail that I had a similar complaint. With a slight groan I admitted that his clever diagnosis was correct, feeling all the time that some terrible disaster was impending, and so it proved to be. For retreating into an inner closet where the drugs were kept, he presently re-appeared with two formidable-looking glasses, each filled with a dark and nauseous draught, which, *nolens volens*, he made us swallow, whilst adding insult to injury, he kept up a continuous peal of laughter, until finally we found ourselves ejected from the door.

Although our interview with the doctor ended so disastrously to us both, we thought we would have another try before giving up all hope of getting away from school, and admitting the truth of the Eastern proverb, *Takdir se lara nahin jata*, or "It is useless to contend against our fate." So my brother scrawled a letter home, saying, that from what he had observed, I was evidently in a very critical condition as regards my health, and unless we were both removed from school at once, our people might fear the worst. This letter, which subsequently was a never failing source of mirth whenever alluded to at home, when first received, was the subject of much comment, alike in parlour, nursery, and servants' hall, and it ended in my father mounting a swift horse and riding post haste to Marlborough College, where he demanded the latest bulletin regarding his *secundus* son. But nobody could make out exactly what he meant. It was true that Number 156 had been treated as an out-door patient, for "headache and pain in his side," but as he had not put in an appearance at the surgery again, it was assumed that he was convalescent. Moreover, on enquiry from the Sergeant, it was discovered that 156 was at that moment enjoying a game at leap-frog, near a point where he could be safely viewed without the disturbance which a personal interview might occasion.

Such an excellent suggestion was at once carried into effect, and my father was led to a window on the left side of the entrance to the old hotel, where he remained until he saw me, as he often afterwards declared, spring at least a foot higher in the air than any other boy. Then, mounting his steed, he rode home again; though perhaps more slowly than he came.

But at length the first holidays of Marlborough College, although I thought they would never come, actually arrived, and on the 20th December, 1843, as I was getting into bed, and as my friend Chang, who occupied the bed next to mine, was taking dire vengeance for all the rough treatment he had received during the past half-year, by singing the doggerel lines, which for some days past had been in the mouths of all the Lower School, one of the maids came into the room and told me that my father had

"YOUR FATHER HAS ARRIVED."

arrived, and would take me home next day. If the ecstatic feeling which came over me could have been prolonged for ever, life would be indeed worth living. The hours since I came to school had seemed so long, and there had been so many landmarks to count them by, that I had begun almost to think there was no such place as home; it must be a mere phantom of my brain. But I should actually see it again to-morrow!

At that time, my school, college, and Indian career appeared like futurity in front. But in after years, when they had all passed, like a dream, behind, I drove down to Marlborough along the road which my father and his embryo school-boys had taken in August, 1843, and I paid a visit to the attic.

The thoughts which crowded on my memory might have affected me perhaps, like those described by the poet, when he stood on the moon-lit bridge, had not the humorous figure of my old friend Chang risen up before me, singing his sarcastic couplet—

> " Good-bye College, good-bye Schools.
> Good-bye all ye Marlborough fools."

CHAPTER IV.

LTHOUGH the first few days of our first holidays were certainly pleasant as the flowers in Eden, the "characters" which followed us and were duly delivered by the postman, bore unmistakable marks of the serpent's trail; for mine consisted of the laconic symbols, "U." and "R.," which would have required the intervention of a Daniel or a wizard to interpret, had not a foot-note explained that "U." implied that my progress as a scholar was Unsatisfactory, and that my conduct had been Reprehensible.

How could a boy be happy with such appendages as these? I began to think that there were too many parson's sons about, and that the world generally would much prefer our room to the honour of our company—as no doubt it would; nor was it any consolation to consider that others were as little regarded as myself.

Just then a bachelor from a neighbouring parish strolled in to tea. He said an "urchin" at Marlborough College called him uncle, and, during his milder, weaker mood had extracted the promise of a cake. "You know," he said blandly looking round, "how good my cakes are; indeed, they are justly celebrated for miles around."

"Then how pleased your nephew must have been to get one," somebody remarked, "for I suppose he does not get much cake at school!"

"But stay!" exclaimed the uncle, as he poured some cream into his cup, "I was going to explain, when you interrupted me; I was about to tell my housekeeper to send the urchin one of the next lot she made, when, much to my surprise, and I may add also, to my sorrow, I received a letter from my nephew, saying that he hoped I would send him five shillings too."

"Well now, I call that very covetous!" another caller cried, "pray, what *did* you do?"

"Do! why, of course, I sent him neither."

Whatever my father and mother may have thought about the sweeping condemnation which arrived from school, it was received with great indignation by the various members of the household, and also in the stables and the garden. My father at once wrote off for further information, whilst my mother, thinking that there must some mistake, made me scrawl a letter to a magician or whatever he called himself, who about that time undertook, for a fee, to delineate character from handwriting. I passed the time until the answers came in considerable alarm, for I knew too well my utter helplessness to defend myself, whatever might be said; and, moreover, there were two high crimes and misdemeanours which I thought might possibly be scored against me.

The first was this: one day my master unexpectedly ordered all his class to bring for his inspection any books of light reading which we possessed; although very few of the boys had any to produce, I happened to have two, and these soon found their way to the master's desk. One was "The Newgate Calendar," which was confiscated at once, with the withering remark that it was clear I contemplated gaining my daily bread on the Queen's highway, or, "As a plough-boy," my master added, after a pause, which was spent in examining my other book, Howitt's "Boys' Country Life." I can hardly suppose that this latter book was "bagged," as we called this phase of robbery at school, for it was given me by my mother. But if it was, and is in the College library now, I should be glad to have it back, and "The Newgate Calendar" too, as they were probably first editions, and worth money now.

The second cause for anxiety was, that in the early College days, before we had a Chapel to ourselves, we used to attend the Parish Church from whose old tower the curfew nightly rang; and there on Sundays, we were put through a fearful ordeal which was called "being Catechised," but which was really little better than a burlesque for the entertainment of outsiders and the College servants, who crowded in the gallery to hear the extraordinary questions asked and answers given.

Q. " The eighth commandment, boy ? "
A. " Thou shalt not steal."
Q. " Do you ever pick or steal ? "
A. " No."
Q. " Do you ever soil your clothes or books ? "
No answer, on which the question is repeated.
A. With trepidation, " Sometimes."

" There ! " exclaimed the Catechist, triumphantly, " you rob your parents, and break the eighth commandment."

" O, you little rogue ! " a saucy damsel, who assisted in the College laundry, cried to me one day, amid the loud laughter of several companions equally saucy. " Oh, you *wicked* little rogue ! " she repeated, pointing to a patch of mud upon my trousers, the result of failing to surmount a fence, " I feel quite ashamed of you, I do ! for robbing your poor pa and ma."

When the answer to my father's letter about the symbols arrived however, no mention of either of these incidents was made, much to my relief. As regards my progress, it explained that I seemed to take no delight in Latin grammar, and as regards my conduct, on enquiry and after much rummaging among black-books, the worst offence they could fairly charge me with was a propensity for damaging trees by " swarming up them ; " a charge which, perhaps,

Lockwood Secundus (No. 156), fairly started "On the Road,"
according to his Marlborough Master's prediction.

would have been omitted, had Darwin's "Descent of Man" been published then.   A postscript added, that I was " very volatile."

The answer my mother got, to my great delight, was most triumphant; for it roundly, and at considerable length, declared that I possessed every virtue which was known to man.   And it had the effect of making everyone about the place, from my old nurse down to the lad who helped in the garden, declare that my friend Chang had much reason to sing, as his adieu,

> " Good-bye College, good-bye schools,
> Good-bye all ye Marlborough fools."

My mother was anxious that this character should be flourished before my masters, but I showed it to my companions on my return to school, and they also consulted the sly magician, much to the satisfaction of both parties.

Besides my instinct for climbing trees, I possessed a great propensity for catching birds, and much of my time during the holidays was passed in alluring birds beneath a sieve propped up by a stick, with a long string communicating to the window or tree behind which I stood concealed.   Small birds were much scarcer in the village then than they are now, for in the Spring nearly every nest was robbed by the village boys, for the sake of a small reward given by the farmers who regarded small birds as their foes.   Consequently I caught very few, but when I did catch one I wrung its neck and roasted it by the saddle-room fire, carefully turning it on an impromptu spit formed with a piece of string. Robins shared the fate of less familiar birds; and when anyone pleaded on their behalf, I considered I had effectually disposed of any misdirected sentimentality on their behalf by quoting the current tradition of the village, " that robins, although apparently so innocent and holy, in reality are fearful hypocrites, if not the most depraved of all the feathered race; as the young ones, on attaining maturity, invariably combine and massacre their parents."

At night I would also surprise the wretched birds asleep in

E

rick-yards, and even the ivy-mantled tower of the Church formed
no certain haven of refuge for their repose, though now I should
view such a proceeding as little less than sacrilege. But boys are
naturally cruel animals; and as I disregarded the aphorism,
"Blessed are the merciful, for they shall obtain mercy," perhaps
many will think I am put out of court when I complain of the
rough treatment which I received at school.

Besides killing the robins, occasionally I would tame them, and
teach them to fly on to my hand, or take bread from between my
lips. Only lately I had two which would fly down from the trees
on to my hand or shoulder on being called, much to the surprise of
persons looking on, and who did not know before how easily their
confidence may be gained. I have determined, however, not to tame
any more, as they are certain to come to an untimely end.

I have never lost my taste for bird's-nesting; but now I am
content to view the eggs *in situ* and leave them there. Nor would
it be supposed that I have lost my taste for enticing birds beneath a
sieve, as such a trap, or something like one, is before my window
now.

In my youthful days, as I have already said, small birds were
scarce, and bullfinches in the village were quite unknown; but
now, from various causes, they abound and do much damage in the
garden; for in the winter the buds of fruit-trees, which form almost
their only food, are no bigger than a small pin's head, and as at
least five hundred are picked off each day by a single bird, a
calculation may easily be made how many *embryo* gooseberries or
plums, a flock of twenty birds, such as I have often seen, will, during
the long winter months, consume.

Frank Buckland had a mistaken notion that these pretty birds do
more good than harm, but I imagine there was no garden attached
to his London house; and had he seen, as I do almost every day,
these rascals climbing up the branches, picking off the buds, and
eventually destroying the trees themselves, he would proclaim their
usefulness no longer.

I can tolerate the presence of any other bird, for with the aid of nets, cotton, and wire guards, I can limit their depredations. But it is impossible to cover high trees effectually with nets, particularly in winter, for the first fall of snow lodging on the net would break the branches down. Consequently there is war between the bullfinches and me. During a deep snow I caught nineteen bullfinches under my sieve, though, perhaps, some may say, "Why not make it a score at once?" But, like the Yankee sportsman— who declared he had killed nine hundred and ninety-nine pigeons at a single shot—I must respectfully decline to record what is not strictly true for the sake of a paltry bullfinch. I put all my captives into cages, where they seemed as happy as the day—plenty to eat and drink, constant society, no rates nor taxes; what more could they possibly want? But a tender-hearted lady opened their prison doors one day and let them fly, with the result that they refused to be enticed again. They build their nests in the trees around my house, in company with countless other birds, and all of them appear to think that my garden belongs to them, and was created solely for their pleasure; and, after all, I should be sorry to live here without them and their never-ceasing melody in Spring.

There is a good deal of hypocrisy often perpetrated regarding the destruction of birds and animals in gardens and elsewhere. That arrant humbug, Friar Tuck, when he grew too fat to hunt, protested, we are told, against anyone hurting the "pretty deer;" and people who have been remorseless bird-nesters in their youthful days will occasionally rate their children for taking eggs. One old lady, whose homilies we often meet with in children's books, and who rejoices, by the way, I think, in the appropriate name of Walker, tells us in pious grief how she rebukes her offspring for chasing a gaudy butterfly; but being asked whether she extends her protection to slugs and snails, she naïvely answers, "No! because they eat the fruit!" indeed, she may be seen dipping such things into boiling water or "sugaring" them with lime. Her infirmity and age preclude her from joining in the chase, but like Waterton's "Daddy Quashi," she

E2

can play a good finger and thumb over strawberries and cream. In fact, she clearly hopes to

> "Condone for faults she is inclined to,
> By damning those she has no mind to."

Besides the pleasure I derived from climbing trees and catching birds, we often had lively scenes within the village. The railroad which joins Oxford with Worcester, passing through the Rectory glebe, was being constructed, and hundreds of navvies found a lodging here. They were a strange rough lot, such as one might expect to meet in a new gold or diamond field abroad. The village constables were powerless to stop any disturbance which they chose to make, and our chief safety lay in their getting high wages for piecework, so, as a rule, most of their buoyant spirits were consumed in a praiseworthy direction. But when the snow lay deep upon the ground in Winter and work was stopped, they passed most of their time in the public houses, from which they would at length emerge well primed for mischief.

It was at such a time as this, when late one night, we were startled by a loud hammering at the Rectory door accompanied by shouts outside, and my father, who was reading by the fire, started up, closely followed by my brother and myself. Somewhat rashly, the door was opened, when a stalwart navvy attempted to effect an entrance, cheered on by comrades from below. My father was about to collar the man, when I handed him an oaken hat-stand which was near, and then all three of us, using this engine of war as a battering-ram, drove it straight against the waistcoat of our assailant, and sent him flying down the stone steps much faster than he came up. Seeing this, and noticing that a crowd of men were coming on, I flew upstairs, and in less than no time handed my father the loaded gun which he always kept in his bedroom in those troubled times. Then the navvies, seeing ours was a formidable stronghold to attack, prudently withdrew, contenting themselves with a burst of boisterous laughter at the discomfiture of their mate.

We complained next day to the contractor, a man of great size and strength, and whom, so the story ran, the navvies feared, as he had won many battles as a prizefighter. He took us down the line to identify our assailant, who however had thought it prudent to decamp.

During the holidays I spent a good deal of my time very pleasantly in the company of the Rev. James Beck,* who, much to my satisfaction, had come to Churchill, the next village, as curate. He possessed what I considered a splendid collection of eggs; and indeed he collected everything which appeared either curious or rare. His house, from cellar to garret, was crammed with specimens of old locks, rings, stamps, turnpike tickets, book-plates, flint implements—nothing came amiss; and reading up information about these things he became quite an encyclopedia of knowledge, so much so that I don't remember ever asking a reasonable question which he could not answer.

He was very popular with us all, as also with our neighbours—rich and poor alike. Through him I acquired a collection of sea-birds' eggs, which I was never tired of exhibiting to the farmers, in fact to anyone whom I could induce to view them. The "Foolish Guillemot," on such occasions, came in for a full share of dissertation; those who were overflowing with hilarity begging me to repeat the bird's name for their amusement; whilst the egg of the Shearwater Petrel would generally elicit the wager of "a guggle"† that I had "fetched it from a hen-roost," until I drew attention to its musky odour.

When I went to India, my brothers, who subsequently followed me, would apply to Mr. Beck for information which no one else could give; and the answer which perhaps is best remembered—for to this day it is often quoted by my brothers, accompanied with laughter and a laconic jerk of the thumb over the left shoulder—is "String 'em up! String 'em up!" the question being, how the

---

* Now Rector of Bildeston, Suffolk.

† An empty snail-shell is called "a guggle" here, and gambling seldom extends beyond "guggle" wagers.

Government would serve the Sepoys who just then were supposed to be killing me?

Tom Phipps, our village postman, when off duty was also my frequent companion, and although he is unknown beyond a few miles from home, he may fairly be added to the list of remarkable men whom this neighbourhood has produced.

Warren Hastings was born at Churchill, as was William Smith, who is alluded to on a monolith raised to his memory as the "Father of English Geology." Their heads made them famous; but Tom's legs have raised him on the pedestal of fame, inasmuch as he has walked a greater number of miles than any other man who ever lived.

His postal duties, commencing in 1840, have taken him over 400,000 miles, of which he has walked 350,000, and had he gone straight on, instead of imitating the pendulum of a clock, he would have walked more than fourteen times round the world on the line of its greatest circumference. An estimate might be made of the number of letters which have been under his charge and delivered, but when we speak of millions the mind fails to grasp such numbers, and it will be more to the point to remark that he has never lost a letter, and however numerous may be the times, during more than half-a-century, he has had to present himself at the post-office, he has never been behind time, or reprimanded for any fault or dereliction of duty. He has to rise, Summer and Winter, between four and five a.m., and when he returns home about eight p.m., and has had his supper and a pipe, he is ready to seek repose, which will enable him to start again next morning.

Tom can count his holidays on his fingers. When I first returned from India, he went with me to London for three days; we put up at the Langham Hotel, and saw all that could be seen in so short a time. But this short glimpse of happiness, derived from a life of luxury and ease, made his post-bag and boots appear so heavy on his return to duty, that he took the hint and has since become somewhat shy of holidays, or anything which might interfere with his present life of long hours, hard work, and contented state of mind.

He has many stories of various curious events, which have occurred on his route during the past half century, and these he tells with much natural humour, and action when gesture is likely to improve the story. But I will only record one event, which illustrates the endurance of the human body and the force of habit.

Tom had gone over his route of twenty-five miles the day of the great snowstorm in January, 1881, and on presenting himself at the Churchill Post-office at seven p.m. found that he was the only officer who had faced the storm. He then had to return home, and on the way he got into a snowdrift which had filled the road breast high. Through this he struggled for an hour, incased in a sheet of ice which fitted him like a suit of armour; but at length he got through the drift. At that point there is an outlying cottage, the inmates of which, hearing him call for help, ran out, and, as they told me afterwards, found the postman·very nearly "cast away." They assisted him to his house, which was close by, and there his clothes were cut off him, and he was lifted into bed, where he remained apparently unconscious of all that was going on around.

Commodore Wilks tells a story of a sailor who fell from a yard-arm upon the deck, and everyone thought the man was dead; the usual restoratives having been tried in vain. At length the grog-bell rang, and then the man opened his eyes and requested that he might be furnished with his share.

The clock striking at the usual hour had a similar effect on Tom, for hearing it he sprang up, put on his private clothes—his uniform suit had been cut to shreds—and going a different road to that which had caused him so much trouble the previous night, he presented himself, much to the astonishment of the postmaster, at the usual hour. He was ordered to return, as no mails had come; and indeed he needed rest, as his hands were frost-bitten and covered with large blisters. The nails also fell off his fingers, and to use his own expression, "they never came in any form again."

Tom often declares that he loves his Queen and Country; and I think we may fairly add that Her Majesty, or at least the Post-office, has no more efficient servant in his humble line as "rural letter-carrier." I was in the Riviera at the time of this great snowstorm, but when I returned to England in the Spring, Tom's narrow escape was still a nine days' wonder in the village.

A deep cutting, thirty feet deep, which divides my farm, was quite half filled with drifting snow, and the railway ganger told me he hastened to the next station and reported the line as "blocked;" but when the first train came in the engine-driver told him to get up into the guard's van behind.

"What's the use of that? I tell you you can't get on."

"Get up behind!" the driver said sharply, "and I will soon show you whether it is blocked or not."

The ganger did as he was told, wondering what would happen. The driver, putting on full speed, ran at the drift and got on as far as he could, then reversing his engine, went back some distance, and at it he went again and again, until at last he got right through. The ganger told me afterwards, that when he saw the snow flying about on all sides, in what he considered a terrific manner, he hung on as best he could to the guard's van, expecting every moment would be his last. "But," I said, "the driver must have known what he was about, and probably had been at that game before."

SKELETON OF THE MAMMOTH. (*Nine feet high*).

In this cutting large quantities of Mammoth's bones were found and sold for beer to anyone who cared to take them away, and thinking I might do a good stroke of business if I could find gravel near the surface, one winter day I took a gang of men who then were out of

work, and sank some shafts, the ganger of the railway being with
me. Whilst we were in the midst of the work, a lady and gentleman
rode up and anxiously enquired what we were all about; and whilst
I was turning over in my mind how I could give a reply in the fewest
words, the ganger cut in and said, " We are trying to strike ile!"

There is much native humour in our village, and native genius
too, though the scanty supply of words the labourer knows presents
a formidable barrier across his road to knowledge. But although
such fine words as primeval and *employé* may at present be absent
from the labourers' vocabulary, the schoolmaster is abroad; the
County Council is instructing us, and the time apparently is coming
when the ploughboy, as he turns the furrow, instead of enjoying
that happy state of mind " thinking about nothing," will work out
square roots and attempt to solve the problem, " Why the pebbles
he throws out of the boulder clay are water-worn, and how they got
there;" but it will be painful work, for nature never intended the
brain and body to work hard together.

During the deep ploughing lately going on at Kingham Hill, a
large skeleton was unearthed, which, judging from the rusty weapons
lying near, savants pronounced to be that of a Roman soldier, thus
fulfilling a prophecy uttered nearly two thousand years ago :—

> *Scilicet et tempus veniet, cum finibus illis*
> *Agricola, incurvo terram molitus aratro,*
> *Exesa inveniet scabra rubigine pila,*
> *Aut gravibus rastris, galeas pulsabit inanes,*
> *Grandiaque effossis, mirabitur ossa sepulcris.* *

About the same time that the skeleton was found, some workmen
turned out of the blue lias clay close by, the bones of a huge
fish-lizard, which could easily have snapped up any human warrior
coming in its way. Had these bones been found in the dark ages, or

* " The time shall come when the farmer, who occupies the land there, shall find rusty weapons, and shall
wonder at the size of the bones turned up by the ploughshare." My friend, Mr. George Phillips, owns a good
deal of the land on Kingham Hill, and the Poet writes :—
> *"Ergo inter sese paribus concurrere telis,*
> *Romanas acies iterum videre Philippi."*

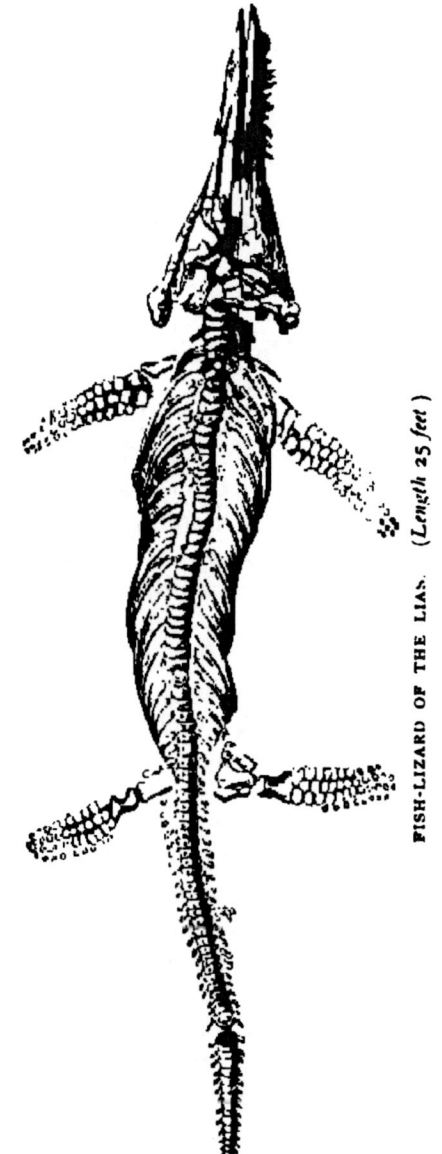

FISH-LIZARD OF THE LIAS.　(*Length 25 feet*)

only one hundred years ago, it is not unlikely that we should have a legend in our village about a dragon, which long had kept the country in dismay, until killed by a knight who also perished in the encounter. But geology has dispelled many of the myths of days gone by.

Words to the above effect, though, I fear, in imperfect English, were scattered around me when I formed the centre of a group of men viewing the bones *in situ*, and growing eloquent, I referred to the Roman occupation of England, of which my audience had no previous knowledge. I went still further, and made some crude remarks about primeval man, who in very ancient days had occupied the hill where we were standing; this also was news, as my companions had never heard of such a gentleman before. I was able to illustrate my remarks by exhibiting a picture of a railway cutting, where the bones of primeval man were found; and I pointed to an *employé* with a pipe in his mouth, perched on the summit of the bank to show its height.

What pleasure there is in diffusing knowledge which is appreciated by an attentive audience; and looking round with feelings of satisfaction, I asked what they thought about it all? The spokesman of the party thanked me for my lecture, and speaking for his mates, he said that whilst they felt sorry that the dragon had killed the ancient warrior, their spirits revived when they saw that primeval man *enjoyed his 'bacca* apparently with the same relish as we do now.

Few of us regret that Great Britain is an island; the surrounding seas present a formidable obstacle to hostile nations, but at the same time many strange and beautiful forms of life, which otherwise might visit us, are kept away. In India, almost every day I saw some new beast, or bird, or flower; and it was well worth keeping a sharp look-out at all seasons of the year, for even on Christmas Day a cuckoo might be sitting silent in my garden, or swallows be seen leisurely circling round undisturbed by domestic cares. Perhaps, in a gloomy tamarind-tree a huge horned-owl would turn his sleepy eyes below, or a colony of egrets, or night-herons, be selecting a home in some of the other trees, whilst an eagle, with its nest close by, would be contemplating my poultry yard.

When the cool weather was approaching in October, the air was full of sounds agreeable to anyone who is fond of watching birds; storks and cranes were hastening to their feeding grounds, and pelicans, just arrived from a journey across the Himalayan mountains, would be prospecting the surrounding country a thousand feet above me, ready to pounce down on any pond or lake likely to hold fish. Then there were flights of waders, whose name is legion, and the ruddy shield-drake, so rare in England, coming from its breeding-grounds in the highlands of Thibet by tens of thousands. When I think of the birds of India, so many recollections start up before me that I must curb my enthusiasm by remarking, that in our village here a *rara avis* is seldom seen, even by the best observer, and during a decade they may be counted on the fingers. One day I saw a bird carrying a mouse

THE GREAT GREY-STRIKE.

which dangled from its claw, and I wrote a post-card in Latin to Mr. Fowler, announcing that it could be no other than the Great Grey - Strike. This brought my correspondent down from Oxford, and after diligent search he found the bird, and wrote to the following effect, though, of course, in much more elegant and polished language,

" Rara avis quam vidisti videlicet Lanius excubitor est."

During the time I was at school, an unique specimen of the Andalusian Quail was shot at Cornwell, about a mile from here, and as it was pronounced to be a highly interesting addition to the list of British birds, Yarrell and Morris figured it. But a few days back, whilst looking over more recent books on Ornithology in Mr. Fowler's house, I find there is a proposal to expunge it from the list. I could not quite make out the reason why, but it appeared that some doubt exists as to the bird having been a genuine wild one. I knew Webb, the keeper who shot it, very well, and he pointed out to me the place where it flew up, whilst the Cornwell coachman, who ended his days in a cottage opposite my house, told me that he remembered taking it from the keeper's bag directly it was brought home.

Not long ago Mr. Penyston, the present owner of the estate where the quail was shot, kindly invited me to see another bird which had been picked up in a moribund condition in his park. He said a naturalist at Cheltenham called it a Dusky Petrel. As this also would have been almost an unique English specimen,

I paused in wonder at the strange coincidence which, *primâ facie*, seemed to bring two rarities to one estate; and although my ignorance regarding petrels is profound, armed with the best authorities I had, I hastened to Mr. Penyston's house, where I measured, weighed, and scrutinized the bird, and then came to the conclusion that it must be a specimen of the Manx-Shearwater—comparatively a common bird. But there it is, in Mr. Penyston's collection, for others more expert than I am to examine.

About the same time the Andalusian Quail was killed, Mr. Lyne, a gentleman in the neighbourhood, shot a Roller. I had heard of this bird and longed to see it when a boy — before this lovely species became familiar to me in other countries. I did not know where Mr. Lyne lived; but a few days ago I was walking through a neighbouring town, and passing an open door, I saw a stuffed Roller in a case standing in the hall. I rang the bell, and said, "Mr. Lyne or his representative lives here!" My surmise proved quite correct, and much to the surprise of the man who arrived in answer to my

THE ROLLER.

summons, I exclaimed, "Everything comes to those who can afford to wait; I have been waiting for nearly half-a-century to see that bird!"

It is much to be deplored that all strange, gaily-coloured birds are killed directly they reach our shores, for if allowed to stay, they would afford a pleasing adjunct to our scenery.   But this is a subject that has already been well thrashed out, with hardly any good result whatever.   I was standing with a loaded gun by our brook last week, when a pair of sea-gulls came flying by, only a few yards

THE ANDALUSIAN QUAIL.

above my head.   My companion was most anxious that I should shoot them.   I sternly turned on him and asked what would be the use of the birds when slain?   This was a question which he completely failed to answer.

When I was a schoolboy I would stand in the cold for hours,

waiting, if possible, to kill a heron ; but now this bird may be seen unmolested in my meadows, and two pairs built their nests and reared their young close by, at Daylesford, where the keeper tells me he hopes they will remain and form a heronry. At the same time, I can quite sympathise with anglers who object to herons, for a few years ago I dug a small pond, about fifty yards in circumference, with an island in the midst, and through it a stream of water ran ; here I made a stew to keep gudgeons handy, when I required them for bait. There must have been at least a hundred in the pond up to a short time ago, and then the herons found it out, with the result that last time I went there for bait, every fish was gone.

In former days many birds were killed by flying against the telegraph wires, which ran alongside the railway through my farm, and once during a deep snow, my father asked me to shoot some partridges for certain festivities which he was giving. In the first field I entered, a covey rose, and on crossing the railway three birds flew against the wires and were killed, whilst a fourth settled and ran beneath the snow as though to hide, and on going up I caught it. I at once returned home and presented my father with two brace of partridges and a riddle, which he failed to answer till I told him what had happened.

Whilst on the subject of birds, I must not forget that we may have too much even of a good thing, and so I will conclude with a brief sketch of the birds which look on my garden as their own. In the Spring almost every bush and tree contains a nest. The Sparrows are on the alert directly the migrants come, and they proclaim a temporary armistice among themselves, after the fashion of the Afghans, in order to attack the new arrivals, for whose accommodation I have put up comfortable, dry, unfurnished apartments, with the great advantage that they are all rent free. The Redstarts put in an appearance among the first which come, and then the sparrows edge up and insult them in every way, evidently sneering, and demanding information why they have invaded a place where they are not wanted. A single cry of disapprobation causes a host of birds to assemble to see the fun, and the new comer is obliged to beat a hasty retreat from the confines of the garden. But in my orchards the Redstarts are not so much molested, and can rear their young in safety as a rule, though on one occasion I found a hen-bird killed upon its nest and eggs by a Tom-tit, which had taken a fancy to the place, and not being able to drag the dead bird out, had built another nest on the top of its victim. When I appeared on the scene it was sitting on five eggs, thinking, perhaps, with Charles IX. of France—

> " Fragrance sweeter than the rose,
> Rises from our slaughtered foes."

A pair of Hawfinches, much to my satisfaction, took up their quarters in my garden. At first the sparrows assembled in force,

THE HAWFINCH.

and some of the bolder spirits tried to turn them out; but a few furious blows administered over the head and shoulders of the aggressors made them retire in confusion, and clearly demonstrated that no humbug would be tolerated; and now the hypocrites, when they see the Hawfinches approach, assume a sanctified demeanour and attempt to sing, "What a good and pleasant thing it is, brethren, to dwell together in unity ! "

The migrants appear in my garden each succeeding year, so far as I can judge, without any addition to their numbers, although their tendency is to increase in geometrical ratio, and fill the earth and sky. If a Cobden or

Bright. could increase their supply of food, as in the case of man, perhaps they would increase likewise, with this advantage over the lords of creation, that they would not be clamorous for work.

When we catch a minute summer-fly, place it under the microscope and see what a perfect little flying machine it is, such as no art can imitate; and when we consider that a thousand millions of these marvellous things are required for the daily bread of the Swifts alone which visit England, we may exclaim with Meer Amman; "*Subhana-llah! Kya sani 'hai*," "The Great Creator: what a wonderful artificer He is!"

F

CHAPTER V.

UT the short first Christmas holidays of Marlborough College soon came to an end, and knowing what was before me I returned with a heavy heart to school, where I found things had by no means improved since I was there before. My master eyed me when I went up to class with no look of love, and soon proceeded to apply his cane to my back, which had hardly healed from the bruises it had received before. I would have run away had there been any hope of keeping away, but several boys had made the attempt, and after wandering about the country for some time, were caught, brought back and flogged. I had not the faintest idea what the Latin grammar was all about, and as no one made the faintest attempt to explain anything, I gave up all hope of understanding it, and passed my time during school hours in other ways than acquiring classical knowledge.

The Spring was coming on, and I turned my earnest attention to that branch of natural science, which treats of the nests and eggs of British birds. We were fortunate in having the run of Savernake Forest, and my happiest time at school was passed in the forest, or by the banks of the Kennet, though our play-hours were so short we

THE KINGFISHER.

F2

could not wander far away, and it was difficult to find a bush or hedge which had not been already explored by oologists quite as eager as myself.

Kingfishers' eggs were highly prized but very seldom found. The bird as it flew by, leaving an apparent line of blue behind, and its fresh eggs, more exquisite than pearls, we ranked with the most beautiful of created things. Even in the East, where lovely species are common in many parts, I never found with them that familiarity breeds contempt, for up to the time when I bade adieu to India, the sight of pied Kingfishers hovering over the Ganges, and other brilliant kinds, gave me as much pleasure as their English cousins did, generally—not always perhaps—at school.

Chang, my partner in eggs, and I had been probing the Kennet banks one day, and spying a likely-looking hole, we cautiously approached it, when suddenly a Kingfisher flew out, nearly in our faces. We went almost wild for joy, and poor Chang for some time seemed to fear impending dissolution, for his almond eyes portruded as we may imagine a shipwrecked sailor's would when he sees a distant sail, "There goes the old Kingfisher," he cried, " I'll take my dying oath," and for some time had any one come strolling by and seen us there, he might fairly have supposed that what little sense we possessed before had utterly departed now, for we sprang into the air, and rolled upon the ground, executing a kind of *pas de quatre* upon our backs, in anticipation of the prize of eggs in store for us, located in that hole.

At length we grew more calm, and thrust in our arms to draw out the expected prize. But the nest contained young birds, and the sleeves of our jackets acquired a most horrible odour, which, as there was no such thing as changing clothes at school, we found impossible to eradicate. Chang looked unutterable things, and so did I, as I said good-bye to all our hopes. The boys who sat on the same bench with us in school showered volumes of execration and abuse upon our heads and arms, which my friend received as he always did, very coolly. But I, who took foul words very much to heart, woefully rued the time when we saw the old Kingfisher fly out.

The rustics in the neighbourhood soon found out that birds' eggs possessed commercial value; and on market days they would assemble at the corner of the town not out of bounds, and expose their wares for sale, whilst we, expecting to find them there, directly we were released from school had an exciting race in order to get first pick of anything curious or rare. I was very fleet of foot, my heart was also in the race, and these combined generally secured me first or second place. On arrival at the gates we had to turn a very acute corner of the road towards the town, and seizing the iron railings we swung ourselves round, with hardly any abatement of our headlong speed. On reaching our goal where the rustics stood, we took a rapid glance at every nest exposed to view, and I soon became very expert in detecting any egg worth buying. But fraud was often rampant and spurious goods were brought. For wherever there is demand there is pretty sure to be supply.

On my table is an heirloom, in the shape of a small oil-lamp, which when the century was young, my father, after performing the grand tour, brought back with him from Pompeii; and in my youthful days it was often the subject for a lecture, which I listened to with great interest not unmixed with awe. The sudden burst of the volcano; the terror of the people who lived below. What a tale that lamp could tell if it could only speak! Perhaps it lighted up the face of some early Christian who had listened to St. Paul. And after lying in the ground for nearly two thousand years, had found a resting place in our village here. Regarding its genuineness of course there could be no doubt, for there was the round hole made by the pick-axe which unearthed it.

In after years when I was performing the grand tour myself; on arrival at Pompeii, my guide with a mysterious air, drew out the exact counterpart of my heirloom, evidently cast in the same mould, probably at Birmingham, for there was the same round hole. "Cosmogony, and the creation of the world," rose up before me, as

I thus addressed my guide, "Friend, I remember having seen something similar before." And much to his disgust I told him of my heirloom.

The egg vendors also soon found out what eggs were in great demand, and armed with an abnormal pullet's egg, one fellow would cry out :

"'Tis Owl's, 'tis Owl's, I sware 'tis Owl's," or holding a Lark's egg in his hand would say :

"'Tis Cuckoo's."

"Cuckoo's, indeed! Pray how do you know 'tis Cuckoo's ?"

"How do I know 'tis Cuckoo's ? Why, because I see the old burd."

"See the old bird! Oh, come now, that's not likely."

"I know I did see the old burd then, and he *were* a-holler-ing !"

"OWLS."

"Hollering, and what was he a-hollering ? "

"What were he a-hollering ! Why Cuckoo, Cuckoo, to be sure ! "—after a pause: "What else should he be a-hollering ? "

But it would'nt do ; and the vendor getting exasperated at the chaff going on around, vowed vengeance on my head, if he could catch me. But his thick boots, like anvils on his feet, gave him very little chance of coming near me in a race.

At last, finding he could not impose on us, he would favour me with a sleepy smile as I greeted him with : " Well, Owls old fellow, and pray what have you got for us to-day ? "

Another egg vendor was "Monkey" Davis, but he never appeared unless he had something good, such as Sparrow-hawk's or Kestrel's eggs for sale. Although as his sobriquet implies, he was not handsome; he was a tall, strong fellow, with a face of great determination, and had his lines been cast in suitable positions, he might perhaps have raised himself to fame by deeds of derring do. But here, so the story ran, he was merely a desperate poacher who never turned his back upon a foe.

Nothing in the shape of live-stock which inhabited the forest was passed by " Monkey " Davis; and in very early days he used to supply the school with squirrels, dormice, rabbits, hardly anything with fur or feathers came amiss; and these we used to keep in a corner between the covered play-ground and the fives-court. The bigger boys must have been about the usual rabbit-keeping age, although they appeared like giants in my eyes, and they soon managed to get quite a large menagerie there. This as time went on, became a nuisance when the wind blew over it towards the school, and really I don't know how it came about that the menagerie was ever allowed to be erected. Perhaps the masters were not aware of its existence until the zephyrs told them, and then it ceased at once.

"Monkey" would also catch badgers, and put them in a sort of cub on market days, and charge a fee for anyone who wished to test the metal of his dog. One day when I was standing near, a dandyfied young farmer came strolling by with a ferocious-looking dog fastened to a chain; and no sooner did the animal scent the tainted gale, than it made such tremendous charges in the direction of the cub, that its owner found difficulty in restraining it. He was invited to let loose this candidate for honours. But the dandy said it would certainly kill the badger in a moment. " Oh, never mind," the " Monkey " said, " so long as I get my shilling." The dog was accordingly let loose, and away it went swift as an arrow from a bow. On getting inside the cub however it gave an unearthly yell; and darting out, tore across country as hard as it could go with its tail between its legs, followed of course by a roar of laughter, whilst the farmer looking very foolish, swore that he would shoot it directly he got home.

Many years after, when I was at home from India on furlough, I met "Monkey" Davis in the forest, and when, for old acquaintance-sake, a coin passed from my hand to his, he pulled out of his capacious pockets, a squirrel and a dormouse, which he begged me to accept. A straw shows the direction of the wind; and as this proffered *quid pro quo* was quite gratuitous, when I said good-bye, leaving my friend in possession of his treasures, I could not help exclaiming, that although in the great struggle for existence he probably had been led to perform some doubtful deeds, I felt sure he was an honest, generous chap at heart.

Another man we knew as " Fur-cap." But as he was lame, a youthful assistant followed in his wake to climb the trees in search of nests. From him I purchased eggs of the Hawfinch, and Water-rail, which ultimately I presented with many others to the Oxford Museum when I went to India. The owner of the forest let us roam about it as we pleased, and "Fur-cap" and his tribe would mask their depredations on the game, under pretence they were merely collecting eggs for us.

It was a gala-day when the Marchioness of Ailesbury, accompanied by out-riders and other forms of state, paid a visit to the School. She used to drive down the "middle path," which, so tradition ran, was reserved for royalty alone, and then a deputation, headed by the best looking prefects, having

" FUR-CAP."

carefully removed their caps, would approach the lady and demand that the great honour she had done us by coming there, should be commemorated by a holiday. Then having gazed at the fair occupant of the carriage and her parasol, which also did duty as a whip, we strolled away to the space outside the pantry door, where "Long Tom," the footman, was regailing the out-riders with "College Ale," amid the chaff of some of the bolder spirits, who enjoyed the grimaces which the ale produced.

One day whilst rushing out of hall in a desperate hurry to go birds' nesting, on turning a corner I got entangled in "Long Tom's" legs and sent him flat upon his back, as he was bringing in the writing master's breakfast on a tray. The tea, the milk, the toast, and eggs came like an avalanche upon him, and as I fled I heard him shouting out : "You've upset the whole concern."

When I paid a visit to Marlborough, after my return from India, I found the "King-Oak" in the forest with a railing round it, with a view to save it from destruction, but in my time, we used to cut off pieces and form them into small crosses, and what we called "baccy stoppers." This latter name was soon passed on to the prefects, who had strict orders to report any boy caught smoking.

Nelson risked an encounter with a polar bear, in order that he might send the skin home to his father, and I "cut roll call" one day in order to get as far as the "King-Oak" to purloin a piece of wood, in order that I might send a small cross to my mother. How I laboured at that work of art, and when I sent it home, I pictured to myself the great delight with which it would be received. I thought at least it would be put under a glass case, with a suitable inscription. When however I got home myself, I found it stuffed away with a lot of "rubbish," and a skein of worsted wound round it. All I could exclaim was, "Oh, fancy!" And my mother seeing how much aggrieved I was, acknowledged that she was wrong. It is wonderful how children take such small things as this to heart, and parents should always be on the *qui vive* about them.

The porous subsoil of chalk, which lies beneath the Marlborough Downs, as every farmer knows, is favourable to sheep, and the great fair which was held close to the College grounds, was attended by dealers who came from all the country round.

In our village here, where much of the subsoil is boulder clay, foot-rot requires the shepherd's constant care; for although I have little doubt that all our farm-yard animals are descended from those domesticated in Abraham's time, selection and survival of the fittest have not yet changed the natural repugnance of the sheep's hoof to anything but dry or rocky ground, such as their progenitors enjoyed on the Himalaya mountains and elsewhere. Indeed, if we left our flock unattended for two, or at the most three years, not a single animal would have survived the combined ravages of foot-rot and the progeny of the beautiful breeze-fly. But on the chalky downs near Marlborough the case is different I believe, and when I was at school, Farmer Beauchamp of this village was annually deputed by my father and other land owners, to drive down to Marlborough fair and make large purchases of sheep, free from the evils which give us so much trouble.

Whilst talking yesterday to one of the old Rectory servants, of whom I am glad to say several are still residing here, she asked me if I remembered a certain hamper which Master Beauchamp took down to the "iron railings" for me nearly half-a-century ago. Of course I did! I should be as likely to forget my name or dwelling place, and I was beginning to describe its shape, and size, and colour, when the old lady cut in and gave minute details, which I never knew or had forgotten, relating from the time when the farmer knocked at the Rectory door, announcing his intended visit to Marlborough, down to the moment when the basket was deposited by her hands in the farmer's gig. Some natural tears the old lady also shed recalling happy days, but wiped them soon, for although Master Beauchamp has long been gathered to his fathers, no one who knew him can talk about him without laughing.

During Napoleon's wars he was drawn for the militia; and his well-known figure, leaning on his shepherd's crook, beneath the "stock trees" on the village green, was pretty sure to draw idlers round to hear him retail stories of his " soldiering " at Oxford. As he was barely five feet high, though quite that measure round the waist, no uniform could be found to fit him. At last a pair of military trousers, with a corresponding long-tail coat, were produced, and to show how they were made to fit, he would raise his extended palm above his head, and bring it sharply down upon the crease opposite the elbow of his other arm, exclaiming, " Why, they cut off as much as that, *I'll warrant*," amid the loud laughter which was sure to follow. Then, at the earnest request of his audience, he would give further details of his military career, which, like his trousers, was soon cut short. For according to his own account, the commanding officer, calling to the sergeant and pointing to him, in angry tones cried out, " There, take that fellow away, and send him home or anywhere you like, so long as he keeps out of my road, for I can't abear the sight of him."

Only those perhaps, who have been hungry, more or less, for eight long years, as I was, will understand why that basket should dwell upon my memory. When the sheep-fair came round the following year, we hoped that a similar hamper would appear. With mingled hope and fear we went from time to time to see if Master Beauchamp had demanded admittance at the " iron gates," but being disappointed, my brother and I determined to pay a visit to the fair next day ; as perhaps the things had come, but by some oversight had been forgotten. Accordingly we went ; and almost the first thing we saw on arrival on the Downs was the farmer's familiar figure, inspecting a pen of sheep and deeply engaged in striking a bargain with another dealer standing by.

On going up he recognised us and shook us warmly by the hand, whilst we felt happy at seeing anyone from home. But no mention was made of any hamper, and as we were too shy to ask point-blank, our interview was soon cut short by the other man abruptly turning round, and demanding information as to whom we were and what we wanted. To this our friend replied, that we were the youthful sons of the parson in the village where he lived.

" Sons of your parson ! " cried the other, " Sons of your parson ! " he repeated with a shout. " Then they must treat us both, and come forthwith to the nearest public house, and give us some gin and water."

This remark was thought so very funny by our friend, that he bent his body forward as far as his figure would allow, pressed his clasped hands between his knees to prevent his falling to the ground, and with protruding eyes turned heavenward, he exhausted himself with laughter. But before he had recovered his original position, both my brother and I had slunk away.

The captain of the set to which I belonged at school, was an overgrown lad with a very sportive turn of mind, who although he found the same difficulty as I did in mastering the Latin grammar, and consequently was always at the bottom of his class, was regarded as quite an oracle, whose decision must be conclusive, when we referred knotty arguments to him, regarding the orthodox way to hold a gun or reins, or the way to train up a cur. I always had some animal to ride at home, and I could generally manage to hold my own in our chief topic of conversation—sport, both in and out of school without confusion, and on one occasion, when I and another boy had a dispute as to which of us was the best rider, it was agreed that each should write to the huntsman of the respective packs located near our homes, and hear what he had to say upon the subject.

Accordingly at the dictation of the captain, whilst half a score of other boys stood by to throw in suggestions here and there, I scrawled a letter to the celebrated Jim Hills, of the Heythrop hounds, who knew me very well by sight, as he and his brother Tom, of the Surrey hounds, and who was an old friend of my father's, would occasionally come over to the rectory, and have luncheon there. In due time a favourable answer to my letter came, whilst my rival's letter remained unnoticed. As this was put down to the negligence of the post office, my rival challenged me to shew my skill compared with his, during the fair, where thirsty souls would let us have a ride upon their nags in exchange for beer.

Accordingly, attended by our respective supporters, we appeared on the Marlborough Downs—It must have been sometime subsequent to my friend Beauchamp's visit—and selecting two rough looking nags, with due ceremony we mounted, and trotted up and down amid much conflicting criticism. The captain said the proper test was to see how far we could surmount obstacles on horseback; and accordingly he led us to a formidable five-barred gate, which I would have much preferred to climb over on my feet. Just as the captain was giving the word to start, a fearful scream was heard to proceed from an old woman in a red cloak, with a basket of eggs upon her arm, who stood in the middle of a group of outsiders looking on. This sounded like a reprieve to my ears, for I felt certain I should break my neck. But the captain looked sternly round, and asked what the old woman was making all that row about, whilst she evidently confident of holding her own in repartee, declared that we both would certainly be killed.

"Killed!" indignantly exclaimed one of the other lads who was not riding, "Why, missus, don't you suppose we go out hunting when we are at home?"

"*Hunting*!" the old lady cried, looking her interrogator all over. "*Hunting*!" repeated she. "No! not unless it may be a cat or a mouse in your ma's kitchen."

Amid the loud laughter which followed this withering retort, the owner of my nag, who was very drunk, ordered me to dismount, as he intended showing us how we ought to ride. But no sooner did he get up on one side then he tumbled over flat upon his back upon the other, to the great enjoyment of the crowd, and when he regained his legs, which he did with difficulty, he declared that such an exhibition was worth money, and he began going round to collect subscriptions in his hat. This of course had the effect of making the crowd disperse, and as our captain was among the first to go, both my rival and myself were not long in following his example. Judging by my own feelings, and the faces and demeanour of my friends, there is no doubt that the old lady in the red cloak had completely routed us. The allusion to the cat, the mouse, and the kitchen, contained so much element of truth, and made us feel so very small, that some time elapsed before we regained our spirits, and alluded to the subject of sport again.

But my mind had been much exercised by reading Cooper's novels. The noble character of Hawk-eye made me long to be a trapper; and when I got sufficient money to buy a trap, I at once commenced a little poaching on my own account. Having also purchased a small plasterer's hammer to do duty as a toma-hawk, I felt as happy as I could be with an incubus of grammar hanging over me, coupled with a scanty amount of food. The bracing air of the district, which produced a Derby winner in my time, made me also very fleet of foot, and as our play hours were so short, I more often ran than walked, so that in setting out to poach, I felt confident that the lessons I had learnt from Hawk-eye, aided by my heels, would set the guardians of rabbits at defiance.

The goal of my first trapping expedition was an old unused chalk-pit, in a field to the left of the Pewsey road, and having first carefully ascertained that no one was about, I set my trap at the mouth of a hole, which appeared to contain some inmates. But on returning next day, I found that in place of the expected rabbit, I had caught a huge Tom-cat, which I tomahawked at once, and dragged out of the pit. This I considered by no means a bad beginning, and I sat down on the bank, thinking how I should dispose of my prize. My trousers were sadly frayed all round my ankles, where "tucks" had been let-out, and I thought at first I would follow the example of O'Flinn, who "had no breeches to wear, so he got an old cat-skin and made him a pair." As that would not exactly do, I caught up the animal by the tail, and bent my steps triumphantly back to School, regardless of the chaff of everyone I met upon the road. On reaching the "iron railings" however, the detective saw me, and in spite of my protestations, relieved me of my prize.

One of my school fellows used to tell with much humour a long

story, which he declared was confided to him by the detective and
the College cook, that my purloined prize was subsequently served
up in one of the formidable pies, which, when Saturday came round,
was said to contain the scraps which had accumulated during the
previous week.   But as he was fond of exercising his wit, frequently
at the expense of truth, I refrain from retailing here what we at the
time thought a highly entertaining story.

The next time I visited my trap, I found I had caught a Pole-cat,
the only specimen of that animal I ever saw alive, so that the
owner of the chalk-pit had very little cause to complain of my
depredations hitherto.   But at last I caught a rabbit, much to my
delight, and instead of taking it to school I took it to a house on
the Pewsey road, where a woman sold " table beer," and she
agreed to cook it for me the next Saturday, when a half-holiday was
given to the School.

Three other fellows, of the baser sort, and poor grammarians like
myself, to whom I confided my success, at first would hardly believe
my tale, but as they knew I was to be trusted, we all went on
Saturday to the place of rendezvous, where we found the rabbit
cooked, and on the table a quart of beer for which we paid three-
half-pence.   I remember that quart of so-called beer, better than
any other I have seen before or since, as one of my companions, an
over-grown raw-boned lad, took such a tremendous swig at it
directly it was put upon the table, that there was precious little left
to divide among the other three, and I have never ceased wondering
that it did him little injury.   Indeed it seemed to do him good, and
in the table-talk which followed, he was the most brilliant of us all.

The spice of danger added much flavour to our feast, and
afterwards we produced a pack of cards and played at whist until
it was time to go.   One of the party also produced a pipe, which I
remember very well, because our cook brought out a thing she
called a " boa," and hung it over the smoker's head, in order, so
she said, to dislodge certain moths which had taken refuge there.

We often visited this house, and as we never knew the owner's

BATHING PLACE, MARLBOROUGH COLLEGE.

(From a Photo by Seeley, Richmond Hill).

G

name, we always called her " Sir," from the peculiar habit she had of never answering any question until it was repeated, and until she had cocked her head very much on one side, and called out sharply " Sir-r !" But she was most obliging, and as time went on she kept a ferret for me, with which I did some execution in the chalk-pits, always carrying my spoils to her, and having them cooked on gala-days, when time permitted us to reach her cottage.

Regarding the games of early days, we had football, which I loved, and cricket, though our eleven was nothing very grand. We played with Swindon, which was captained by the celebrated Budd of by-gone days. His arms were of enormous size, though he must have been an old man when he played with us. One day I met him with a new bat going to the cricket ground, and he asked me to throw him a ball, as he wished to prove his weapon, and catching it just right, he sent it flying to such a distance that—I was going to say I had to run nearly half-a-mile to pick it up—but it could not have been quite so far as that. He was evidently pleased with his performance, for turning to a crowd of boys now gathered round, he said, " Just to try it you know, Hey ! Just to try it !" Those words seem ringing in my ears even now, and for many a long day I know they were remembered by my comrades, who when they made a successful stroke at cricket, would cry out, " Just to try it you know, Hey ! Just to try it !" and then all within hearing, would re-echo the same cry with laughter.

When the days were wet, we assembled in the covered play-ground, to jump in the long rope ; and this was a favourite game with me. The place was crammed with ropes, all being swung round together, with a hundred boys or so, all jumping and keeping time, which must have presented a very Zoological garden, monkey-house appearance to any outsider looking on. This play-ground was also marked with rings for marbles, and one Hebrew-looking lad was considered a millionaire, because he owned a pocketful of agates.

Then there was the bathing place, where I learnt to swim. But in very early days we only had the Kennet to disport in, and round promontories were erected about a hundred yards above the mill, from which headers could be taken.

BLACK-HEADED BUNTING.

On the other side of the river was a well-wooded swamp, where in the Spring the Black-headed Bunting had its home, and the Reed-warbler would build its lovely nest, supported by slender columns and rocked to and fro by every passing breeze; the Moorhen and the Dabchick were always there, calling in the most exasperating way, as though they felt quite safe from school-boy depredations. I viewed the place with longing eyes, and though I was an indifferent hand at sums, would calculate how much I would " put down upon the nail " to spend half an hour there in Spring, when the poor little birds were busy with their nests. I can't remember that I ever thought they might object to my robbing them, and even the bare idea of leaving a single egg, which ultimately might produce a father's hope or a mother's joy, was scouted in derision, and in fact, to cut short what appears to be getting rather a prosy story, I determined, come what might, to explore that El Dorado.

The best way to get at the place was by going through the mill. But the Miller was a dreadful ogre, and as he often said, he couldn't abear them boys. Swear! Why, so far as I could discover, he didn't know any other words than oaths and imprecations, which he would shower on our heads, and eyes, and limbs. However, I was determined to have some eggs; and so one market day I watched the rascal leave his house and go off towards the town; then, leaving a companion perched on the high bank which overlooked the river, to keep watch and hollo "*Cave!*" if anything went wrong, I slipped through the mill, and soon was busily engaged in filling my cap with eggs. It was nearly full when I heard "*Cave*" repeated many times, and hurrying back I met the Miller on his threshold. The fellow could not have been far removed from a savage animal, for directly he saw me coming he seemed to go stark staring mad, working his arms about like a windmill, and bellowing like a bull. I sprang into the air, and alighted on his chest, sending him over on his back, and then triumphantly sat on top of him, whilst he, like Proteus in the grasp of Aristaeus, tried every artifice to

THE MOORHEN.

get free. He grabbed my cap to get my number, so he thought, but I had become too old a bird for that, and I hammered his fingers with my fists until he let it go; then, springing to my feet, I dashed away. Alas, without my spoils, for all the eggs were smashed.

* Beware!!

CHAPTER VI.

ESIDES the chalk-pits I have mentioned, during the Spring and Summer months I turned my eyes towards the river Kennet, in which I caught some trout; these I cooked over a fire made in some secluded spot. The betraying smoke was a constant source of danger to me as it was to Cooper's Indians, although, after I had set fire to a heap of sticks, I strolled away until the bright embers alone remained. I got caught at last, however, for as time went on, I neglected precautions to avoid surprise, but when the detectives appeared upon the scene my meal was over, and they only saw the fish bones strewn about. Of course the master called me to his desk next day, and duly punished me; entering my crime, as one of lighting a fire out of bounds in order to fry red herrings.

The keepers were always on the watch; but they never caught me, although I had a narrow escape one day, when a man surprised me in a *cul-de-sac*, bounded by some park-railings, but I dashed my foot against a rail, which luckily gave way and let *me* through, though not the burly keeper. This man vowed vengeance on my head, eyes and limbs, whilst loudly lamenting my depredations, and an audience would occasionally gather round, condoling with him, and tendering advice how to circumvent me. One perhaps would raise his eyes, as though in mute surprise that there could be any difficulty, and blandly ask, "Why don't you run arter him kipper?"

"Why don't I run arter him," the guardian of the stream replied, spitting on the ground in sheer disgust after the manner of Orientals, "Why I might as well run arter a greyhound."

In after years, when I went to Haileybury, the Indian Civil Service College of those days, I found the foot races a great institution there. But as I was a dark horse, I was nowhere in the betting, and my immediate friends expressed surprise when they heard I had entered for the "Derby," or "Hundred yards." One of the favourites invited me to have a trial spurt with him, in order to see what I could do. But although I by no means had forgotten the lesson taught me by the Marlborough doctor on the subject of deceit, I thought I might fairly decline to expose my hand by shewing this rival competitor my heels just then. And the result of the trial spurt, which soon got noised abroad, was that I should probably be nowhere in the race.

But I felt confident that if once I got ahead no one would ever catch me: and so it proved to be, for I came in first, and won a gold-mounted racing whip in a presentation case, which was the prize awarded. I ought to have got something much more valuable, considering the amount of money collected for the races. But the system in vogue regarding the purchase of the prizes was utterly bad and scandalous, to use no harsher term. The three stewards went to London to purchase the prizes with a *carte blanche* given —by no one knew whom—to spend as much as they chose upon themselves, after the fashion of the prodigal son, *vivendo luxuriose*, or in riotous living, and they made no secret on their return of having enjoyed themselves, or to use their own words, "In having had their fling" at our expense. I dare say they excused themselves in the words of Tacitus, quoted in Paley's Evidences,

"*Hi ritus quoquo modo inducti, antiquitate defenduntur.*

But this was poor consolation to the prize winners. I also won the hurdle race, and broad jump, getting prizes hardly worth acceptance, but one of these, a hunting-knife, is still in my possession.

William Salmon,* my messmate at College, who was considerably over six feet high, used to express astonishment that his long legs could not carry him over the ground so fast as mine, which were comparatively short, did me. Although I replied he should remain content in having a better head than mine, he resolved to cope with me in the College Steeple-chase, which led over a dug-out place full of water covered with green scum, and surmounted by a railing. Almost the entire population of the surrounding country would assemble there on our gala-day, to share the fun of seeing the athletes fall in, but I could just manage to jump it from bank to bank without getting wet at all. And for several days before the race I used to practice there, in order to find out the best place for taking off and landing on the other side.

Salmon, who was a dandy, having procured the most becoming racing dress his tailor could supply, looked very smart when we all assembled at the starting place, and to use his own expression, he "felt so fit," that he thought he might acquire a little fortune if he only would accept the odds so freely laid against his even reaching the winning-post at all.

"Are you ready?" What an exciting time that was, as every eye was on the starter. "Off!" Away we went, all led by Salmon, who never heeded for a moment that "it's the pace which kills." The water jump was not far off, and by the time he reached it— many yards before us all—no breath remained in his body, in consequence of the terrific pace he had been going. Cheered by the crowd, however, he made a noble effort, but his foot catching in the rail, he alighted on his back in the middle of the water with a tremendous splash, amid the delighted laughter of the crowd. He was assisted out by our much loved Dean,† who when order was

* Gold Medallist, died at Bombay. His executors sent me a very valuable diamond ring, which they said had been left to me by my old messmate as "a token of affection."

† The Rev. W. E. Buckley, an athlete, and scholar of considerable fame. Every one who had the honour of his acquaintance loved and respected him. Died, 1892.

restored, raised his hand for silence, and thus addressed the crowd—

"We must all join in thanking Mr. Salmon for the entertainment he has afforded, and in gratitude I propose that this formidable obstacle shall no longer be known as the 'Water Jump,' but as the 'Salmon Leap.'"

But, returning to Marlborough College. During the entire time I passed at school, the general feeling between the masters and the boys was one of distrust and enmity, and considering that the cane was always on the go, this was only what might naturally be expected; for I doubt whether much love is ever lost between masters of any kind, and those they have assaulted.

When I first arrived in India, a veteran gave me the following advice in which I heartily concur: he said, "Don't strike your native servants, for apart from other reasons, they are sure to dislike you for ever after, and are pretty sure to find some means to injure you."

According to Thackeray, the schoolmaster flogs his own son more than any other boy; but this sounds too horrible to be true. If it is true, such a fellow must have common ancestry with the Fuegian immortalized by Darwin, who dashed his child upon the rocks for dropping a basket of sea-slugs.

"Hey! What? Sea-slugs! I am sure I should never dash my child," etc.

No; not in England where policemen are about; but I should be sorry to trust you on a wild and broken shore in Terra del Fuego.

The tyranny and eccentricities, or what we considered such, of the masters formed subjects for much doggerel rhyme, which will not bear repetition here. Its nature may fairly be described however in the words of George the Second, who, as I have somewhere read, on casting his eye over a lampoon which a certain Bishop had handed to him in order that punishment should be meted out to the obnoxious writer, burst out laughing; and when his lordship, much scandalised, exclaimed, "Surely, sir, you cannot find amusement in such ribald trash," His Majesty, looking supernaturally grave, replied,

"*Mais que non! C'est mauvais, c'est execrable! Mais,*" and here the royal countenance lit up again, "*il faut avouè que le drole a de l'esprit.*"*

One of the masters, when he came upon us unawares perpetrating any peccadillo would exclaim, as he seized us by the hair or neck, "Slippery fellow, I've got you at last!" He also affected a highly-polished satin stock with an iron buckle which fastened it behind, the end sticking out several inches and presenting in the distance a formidable horn or pigtail, and as this from long usage had become much frayed, the boy who sat next to me in school exercised his wit in writing a poem; describing the master's supposed search through the various shops in the town for a new stock of the same antiquated shape and pattern, describing it as "one of the old sort, buckle behind." This description being incomprehensible to the shopmen, various forms of banter, in which the words "slippery fellow" were freely used, filled up the poem, which at last concluded, by a cupboard, fastened by a rusty lock unused for a century or more, being opened and disclosing the long sought for article. On which the joyous purchaser skipped out of the shop, very fast, crying,

> "Slippery fellow, I've got you at last!
> The old sort, buckle behind!"

But, of course, there were some favourites amongst the masters. When I was staying, years ago, in the Riviera; a man came to me and said, "There is an old Marlborough master staying at our hotel, would not you like to meet him?"

Somewhat hastily, I was about to return an answer similar to that which Boswell says Johnson would have given had he been asked to meet Jack Wilks, when checking myself, I sternly said, "What is the master's name?" and hearing that it was Tweed, I

---

* "It is bad; indeed it's really shocking; but we must acknowledge that the rogue has wit."

said, " Oh! that's all right! it will give me much pleasure meeting him ; for although, unfortunately, I was not under him at school, I am sure I never heard his name mentioned except in praise."

But if the masters made guys of themselves, the boys were often not far behind in that respect. I was forced into a shilling grey Scotch-cap, from which the ribbons, put for ornament behind, soon disappeared, and upon this I sat when I was in school. My trousers also usually had one, and sometimes two, frayed lines where tucks had been let out as my legs grew longer ; and upon Sundays the prefects and fifth-form boys appeared at Church in the full ball costume worn by the "mashers" of that time. A long-tail coat, and waistcoat which had one button only, in order to display a white shirt-front kept together by three large jewelled studs like unripe blackberries, and over these was an enormous Joinville tie, such as Lord Scamperdale wore at Jawlyford Court, making him appear " like a goose with an apparatus round its neck to prevent it creeping through gaps and gates." The hair of these " awful swells," as they were called, was plastered down with bear's grease, which gave them a very oily look; and thus adorned, with a blue or red cricketing cap surmounting all, they would promenade the Bath or Pewsey roads, much to the amusement of strangers passing by.

Everyone did his best to look smart on Sundays, even if smartness consisted merely in getting an extra polish to his Blucher boots. But it was a hungry day, no notice being taken of Festivals, though Fast-days were rigidly observed.

Lent was a much dreaded time at school, and certainly there was enough tyranny and humbug mixed up with it to last one for a lifetime. It made me break the tenth commandment, for I envied the lucky fellows who had money and who could lay in a store of food. Two brothers, who sat near me and whose features betrayed their Hebrew origin, would bring out, about Shrove Tuesday, a well-lined purse, and tell us in exasperating detail, the precautions they were taking to drive off the wolf of hunger, whilst the others sitting near longed, of course, to follow their example. On

Wednesdays and Fridays my only food was stale bread washed
down by water from the pump, and we used to search for pig-nuts
to satisfy our craving.   Salt fish occasionally was put upon the
table, but an edict had gone forth that it was not fit for human
food, so no one ever touched it.   I have heard it said that no one
knows who leads the fashions; and certainly I never heard who
passed the order about the fish—masters? boys? or was it evolved
out of our inner consciousness?   But there the order was, and we
small boys could not disregard it, unless we wished to make our
lives a burden to ourselves.

Then we had to attend long services in Chapel, and listen to
dreary sermons which no one but the pulpit orator himself could
possibly enjoy.   But I must not, in justice, omit to mention that
the masters were supposed to share the austerities which they en-
joined on us; this, however, afforded only indifferent consolation.
Indeed, those who are engaged in instructing youth should not be
allowed to fast at all, for a reason that may be illustrated by a
passage which I find in Andrew Lang's translation of Theocritus—

> " Diocleides has not had his dinner, and the man is all vinegar—don't
> venture near him when he is kept waiting for his dinner."

And everyone knows the amusing diary of the Quaker Dr. Rutty,
and the entry, "Snappish on fasting."   Quakers, so far as I have
seen them, are the mildest and best of men, and if they become
snappish when deprived of food, what must those who are naturally
savage be?

I have no doubt however, that the authorities at School when
they made us fast, acted according to their light, but it was the
lucus a non lucendo of the ancients, which may be translated here,
as *a light which makes darkness visible*.   I suppose it was intended
for mortification, as though there was not enough of that about
already.

The river Kennet developed my love for fishing; and since the time
when I broiled trout out of bounds upon the embers, much of my

time has been passed by the brook or river-side, where, even if the fish are not inclined to move, there is always something entertaining going on ; and, indeed, the angler who sets out to cast his lines upon the waters where destiny has usually led me, must do so more in hope

> "To steal from all he may be, or has been before,
>   And mingle with the universe."

than to fill his basket ; for civilization, with its attendant factories and gas, have worked sad havoc with our fish.   But the Geologist-angler, wandering by the Evenlode, if he finds the fishing slow, may speculate on the share which the great ice-age had in making the river thick with yellow mud after every heavy shower of rain, whilst the Windrush on the other side of the Cotswold hills, and only a few miles distant, remains clear as crystal.   He may also attempt to solve three problems : Why the river forms a succession of curves shaped like the letter S ? Why the surrounding land is highest close to the river bank ? and why, although denudation by frost or flood is constantly going on, the banks remain perpendicular on either side, and equidistant from each other.   The mathematician may weigh a portion of the deposit brought down from the surrounding hills, and calculate how many years will pass away before the surrounding water-shed is levelled down ; and the naturalist, if he has observant eyes, may find food for speculation sufficient to last him for a lifetime.

Not long ago I was sitting on the river bank which forms a boundary to my farm, when on the opposite side a water-rat came tearing by as though fear had lent it wings ; and no wonder, for presently a stoat appeared upon the scene in hot pursuit, evidently bent on mischief.   I sat quite still until it had gone by, then there issued from my lips a sound like that of a micro-mammal in distress. The pursuer pulled up at once, and looked my way, as though it would exclaim, " Great heavens, what's that ? " standing on its hind legs to get a better view.   This was evidently satisfactory, for it took a header into the water, swam across the stream, and mounting the steep bank, came in a desperate hurry towards the place where I was sitting; when it got so near that I could have touched it with my hand, a panic seized it, and taking another header got back to the other bank. I stopped it again with the same mysterious sound, and if ever perplexity—hope mixed with fear—was written on the countenance of a stoat, there it was before me. It evidently thought it the most remarkable coincidence which had occurred

STOAT KILLING RABBIT.

during its brief existence, and come what might, it was determined to see it out. Another header, another rapid scramble up the bank for fear it should be late for dinner, when a sudden burst of laughter, which I found impossible to restrain, drove it back again. Twice after that it returned, and there is no knowing how long the game might have continued, had not a farmer who wished to speak to me, appeared upon the scene, and frightened this entertaining stoat away.

The farmer capped my story of what had just occurred, by telling me that on one occasion a stoat drove eight rabbits in succession from the neighbouring Daylesford woods, to the field where he was working, and so disabled them before his eyes, that he was able to secure them all; and there was no knowing how many more additions to his larder might have been supplied in this unusual manner, had not a keeper suddenly appeared and ended the rabbit-hunter's life.

Seeing my basket nearly empty, the farmer invited me to try his portion of the brook, which is situated at a considerable distance from the place where we were sitting. He said, from what he had heard going on that morning, he had reason to believe that large fish were jumping in sheer light-heartedness. I asked if they could possibly be trout, but he replied No! No! he was certain they were not trout, as he had never heard of any there; he felt confident they were "Jacks." So next morning found me with trolling tackle in my neighbour's field, under the impression that the sounds which had attrated him proceeded from other things than fish. I was in the act of adjusting a dead gudgeon on my hook, when suddenly a May-fly, the first I had seen that year, flew by, and I had hardly secured it when a tremendous splash in a corner close at hand filled me with astonishment, as I had never

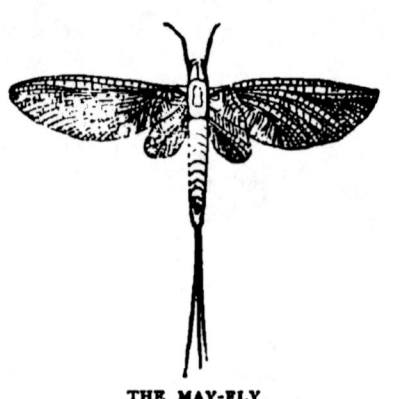

THE MAY-FLY.

heard anything resembling it in the brook before. I quickly changed my tactics, and in almost less than no time a May-fly was fluttering in the corner whence the unusual noise proceeded. It hardly touched the water when down it went and with it my hook stuck in a fish's mouth. I thought for some time that I must have caught a salmon, for the fish behaved exactly as a salmon did in the Usk one day when I was trout-fishing there. It went to the bottom of the stream and there it stopped, until straining my line almost to the breaking point, it suddenly changed its tactics and dashed away upstream as hard as it could go. I followed for some distance, keeping it out of the weeds as best I could, when to my relief it turned and came again into the large corner where there was plenty of sea-room, and there for quite ten minutes it dashed about and every now and then sprang into the air, trying to break my line. But at last it yielded, and dragging it down stream to a convenient place where cattle come down to drink, I slipped my landing-net under it and pulled it triumphantly on to the bank. It weighed five

FIVE-POUND TROUT FROM THE EVENLODE.

pounds, and now, with glassy eye it surveys me as I write.   During the struggle several other fish were jumping round, and directly my first prize was landed, I proceeded to wait on them; and soon four others, though not quite so large as the first, were lying on the grass.

My friend, the farmer, then appeared upon the scene, and was so pleased with my success, that he declared 'he would be-come an angler himself; a threat which I am selfish enough to say, much to my satisfaction, has never been fulfilled.

I must not fail to mention that the field where we were standing was thick with grass just ready for the scythe, and when I pointed to the damage I had done, my friend exclaimed, " Perhaps you don't remember that it was I who carried you up the Rectory steps when first you came to Kingham; and, more than that, my wife, who is now I trust with God, has often told me that she made your shirts when first you went to school. With such bonds of friendship, can you suppose that I could possibly object to your treading down my grass? No! No!!"

> *" Felices ter et amplius,*
> *Quos irrupta tenet copula, nec malis*
> *Divulsus querimoniis*
> *Suprema citius solvet amor die."* *

My progenitors transmitted to me a love of sport. My father used to tell us how, during his holidays, he was always either riding after the Surrey staghounds, or prowling about with his gun. He was supposed to produce a holiday task in manuscript, on his return to Westminster, where he was at school; but, like me, he does not appear to have taken kindly to grammar, for when his master demanded the expected document, he related the following tale of woe :—

His youthful ambition was, he said, to take back a present of game to his master, so accordingly, the day before leaving home he took a stroll with his gun, and after walking nearly all day without seeing either " fur or feathers," suddenly came across a hare comfortably seated in its form and fast asleep. Here was a splendid opportunity, but on searching his pockets, O, horror! he had no wadding with which to load his flint-and-steel gun.

I can quite believe this part of the story, for boys, whether shooting or fishing, are pretty sure to forget some very important item—bait, hooks, wadding—indeed, so far as my experience goes, the only item which a boy can be trusted to produce is " Grub." But however that may be, on this occasion, although my father

---

* " Thrice happy fellows those, whose friendship lasts a lifetime, and whose bonds of union are so great that the bare idea of one complaining because the other has trodden down his mowing grass is scouted as absurd." —*Free translation.*

turned his pockets inside out, the only paper he could find was his holiday task, with hardly a single grammatical mistake, according to his own account. Being on the horns of a dilemma, he rapidly turned over in his mind what on earth he should do; and coming to the conclusion that his master would much prefer the hare to the holiday task, he rammed the document down the barrel and shot at the hare.

I had no idea when I began writing this story down that it would become so long, or I should have hesitated before producing it, and the master must have been unusually good-natured to hear it out; but hear it out he did, and when it ended he curtly called out,

"And where's the hare?"

"O, please sir, I'm awfully sorry, sir, but *I missed it!*" *

As my ancestors, so far back as there is any record of them, appear to have been sportsmen; no wonder that during the hour or so which we were allowed, twice a week, to wander through the town of Marlborough, I spent some portion of my time in flattening my nose against a window where a certain old pistol was exposed for sale. I longed to buy it at the advertised price—five shillings. At last I screwed up courage and scrawled a letter to my mother, saying that I wanted five shillings sadly; and in due time that sum arrived with the remark that I had set a-going much speculation as to the reason why the money was so urgently required. My father supposed it was to purchase the egg of some rare bird; whilst my mother thought perhaps it was to buy a white feather from a sparrow's wing. But it was really to buy that pistol. The shop-keeper ought not to have sold it to me, but he did; and forthwith I and another boy employed our time in casting bullets; but disaster soon commenced. First we poured some of the molten lead into the hollow handle of a shovel containing water, and the steam generated there, shot the lead with tremendous force up to the ceiling, narrowly missing our faces, but it burnt our hands. Then

* This incident, which must have occurred about the time of Waterloo, is perhaps still current at Westminster.

the pistol went off as my companion was looking down the muzzle, and the bullet went through the peak of polished leather which adorned his hat. Again, when I stuck up the ladle as a mark, the bullet, fired true, whizzed round, and returning struck me on the chest. Soon after another boy borrowed this dangerous weapon, and as he was dealing destruction far and wide, the detectives, hearing the unwonted noise, appeared upon the scene, which terminated—not unjustly * I allow—in his being flogged and the pistol confiscated. If that article is in the College museum now, the authorities need have no fear of my ever claiming it, as I claim the books which I have already mentioned.

But I soon found another way to satisfy my love for sport. In my day Mr. Somerset, who kept innumerable white pea-fowl, occupied the farm in the valley on the left, going to the cricket ground, and about a mile along the valley his shepherd lived in a small isolated cottage. This man possessed a gun which he would let me have for a small consideration, and on half-holidays, when I had any money, I often paid a visit to the cottage, and passed an hour or so in shooting sparrows, tom-tits, or any mortal thing which happened to come by. The first bird I killed was a wretched goldfinch, which I kept in my pocket as long as I could conveniently do so, and during school hours I would exhibit it with much pride to my neighbours.

I hope to pay a visit to Marlborough soon, and so vividly are the various scenes impressed upon my memory, that I shall almost expect to see the white pea-fowl, the old gun, and the old man who lent it out. But I fancy they have all long since passed away, as I am talking of nearly fifty years ago. Even young Mr. Somerset, who menaced me with a whip when he caught me standing on the rafters of his barn probing the thatch in search of sparrow's eggs, but released me when he found I plied a useful

---

* Perhaps some will remark that I don't object to other boys being flogged, whilst I cry out myself. Well! it certainly does make some difference. Such is the weakness of mortal nature; and there is this to be said, that the boy not only refused to refund the value of my pistol, but gave me a good licking for lending it to him and getting him into trouble.

H2

trade, has I suppose also disappeared, though at the time I saw every prospect of his remaining there for ever.

It was a happy time when the school broke up for the Summer holidays, as we were free to go pretty well where we liked until we could be all packed off. The small boys of course went last; but we could hear the ringing cheers of those who had already started, and we passed our time in thinking over the happiness in store for us at home, and devising schemes for pleasure.

But the trail of the serpent was always visible when "my character" arrived per post, and was placed like a wet blanket on the Rectory breakfast-table. As I was never taught anything, of course my progress could not be called satisfactory; but during eight long years as the worst crimes which could be scored against me were—The attempted introduction of a dead cat into the school, and the possession of "The Newgate Calendar," I never could understand why my conduct was generally condemned. I am certain I was always ready to do anything I was told, that is, if I knew how to do it, and I would have led a "forlorn hope" had I only received a command to lead it.

Directly I got home I went the round of the village to see all my friends, as I knew every man, woman, and child in it—as I do now; and then I started off to the brook and elsewhere, to see if I could find anything new in the shape of birds, beasts, plants, or fishes.

Had nature endowed me with an intellect coinciding with the sharp look-out I always kept when I took my walks abroad, goodness only knows what I might not have discovered in the vast field of natural history; though doubtless it would have been better had I kept a sharp look-out for grammar, and a correct interpretation of the three concords or agreements in Latin, whilst I remained at school. But there is no accounting for tastes, and as I have already recorded my Indian observations in "The Natural History of Monghyr," I will conclude this chapter with some notes which I made when I found a Pied Flycatcher's nest in Wales. If any think them dull, all I can say is that I am in good company, for the Editor of *"The Field"* said at the time they were very interesting, as this bird had not been previously recorded to build its nest in Wales.

"A pair of Pied Flycatchers have taken up their quarters in a secluded part of the park here, and on climbing up to their nest, which is built in the hole of a small elm tree, about twenty feet from the ground, I found that it contained four blue eggs. I first noticed these birds a week ago, and never having seen the species alive before, I sat down under a neighbouring tree and watched them. I had not sat there long before a squirrel, which has made its dray or nest in a holly bush close by, crossed over to the Flycatchers' tree, and was proceeding leisurely in the direction of the nest, when the birds, which were anxiously watching its movements, attacked it in the most furious and determined manner, screaming violently, and apparently striking it with their beaks. The squirrel seemed to view the attack rather in the light of a joke than otherwise, and kept dodging round and round the tree in order to avoid the blows showered on it, but showing no inclination to retreat until I got up and drove it away. I do not know whether the

THE PIED FLYCATCHER.

squirrel would eat the eggs if he could get at them, but I have found lately several blackbirds and thrushes' nests containing shells of eggs which have evidently been sucked, and I put this destruction down either to the squirrels or carrion crows which abound in the park.

"The Pied Flycatcher is an unmistakeable species, being unlike any other British bird. In the distance, however, it bears considerable resemblance to the common magpie robin of India; and, indeed, when I first saw it, for a moment forgetting the locality, I mistook it for the Indian bird.

"The well-wooded country in this neighbourhood doubtless contains many rare species of birds, but as comparatively few persons take an interest in any but game birds, they remain unnoticed. The park here almost rivals the celebrated Walton Hall in the number and variety of birds. There is a path which separates two ponds about one hundred yards from the house, and here, in a decayed elm tree, a green woodpecker has hollowed out its nest. It is generally supposed that this bird carries the wood which it excavates to some distance, in order to escape detection; but from the number of chips under this tree, one might imagine a carpenter had been at work there with his chisel. The next tree contains two noisy broods of starlings, and on the opposite side of the path two pairs of willow warblers have built their nests in the bank close to each other. Below them again a dabchick and a moorhen, side by side, have reared their young ones, and in the branch of a willow tree, which has fallen into the water, a chaffinch is engaged in building its nest. A few paces further on a third pair of starlings have taken possession of an old woodpecker's hole; and beyond these again a blackbird in a hawthorn bush is sitting upon its eggs. A squirrel has made its nest in a fir tree, the centre of the group; and as the birds and squirrels apparently form a very peaceful and happy family, perhaps my supposition regarding squirrels destroying eggs is an unjust one.

"The Dipper is a very common bird here; under almost every bridge may be found one of these birds nests. There are two wooden bridges over a small trout stream which runs through the park. I found two nests under the first bridge, and one under the second. A brood of five birds has already been reared in one of the nests, and I found the old bird sitting again on four eggs.

The Dipper appears to possess remarkably keen eyesight, and considerable difficulty is found in watching its movements

THE WATER OUSEL, OR DIPPER.

unobserved. Its flight is very rapid and headlong. On several occasions, whilst fishing in the well-wooded trout stream, I have had to duck my head to avoid—at least so I thought—the bird flying against my face, and on one occasion it actually flew against my line. The paradoxical nature of the Dipper is well worthy the attention of the disciple of Darwin. In gesture and nest it resembles the wren; in flight, voice, haunts, and colour of its eggs it resembles the kingfisher; whilst, according to naturalists, its anatomy bears close affinity to that of the thrush.

"Numerous as are other birds, we miss the nightingale, whose antipathy to Wales forms one of the most curious features in the migration of birds. Considering the unrivalled song of the nightingale, it is curious how often the notes of other birds are mistaken for it. Last May, whilst in Palestine—remembering the lines in 'Lalla Rookh,'

> 'And Jordan, those sweet banks of thine,
> And woods so full of nightingales '—

I listened attentively on the banks of the Jordan, but heard nothing which might lead me to suppose that Philomel was there. My dragoman assured me, however, that nightingales were common; but, considering that he pointed out the scavanger vultures as eagles, I did not attach much weight to his testimony.

"In Dr. Johnson's 'Life of Savage,' mention is made of a scheme proposed for the happy and independent subsistence of the improvident poet, namely, that he should retire into Wales and receive an allowance of £50 a year—to be raised by subscription—on which he was to live privately in a cheap place, without aspiring any more to affluence, or having any further care of reputation. This scheme appears to have met with the warm approval of the poet, and ' when he was once gently reproached by a friend for submitting to live on a subscription, and advised rather, by a resolute exertion of his abilities to support himself, he could not bear to debar himself from the happiness which was to be found in the calm of a cottage, or lose the opportunity of listening without intermission to the melody of the nightingale, which he believed was to be heard from every bramble, and which he did not fail to mention as a very important part of the happiness of a country life.' It was unfortunate that the poet should have rested his hopes on almost the only common British bird not found in Wales, and had Dr. Johnson been anything of a naturalist, he would probably have mentioned this incident in his ' Vanity of Human Wishes.' "

CHAPTER VII.

OW that the agricultural labourer has obtained a vote, the eyes of politicians are turned towards him. Orators whose tall hats proclaim that they hail from the metropolis, have interviewed us here, and attempted to demonstrate, not only to ourselves, but to all the world, that village life is " remote, melancholy, slow." No excitement, no music hall, not even a hurdy-gurdy, by whose enlivening strains we might tread an occasional measure with our friends.

But this is merely a Londoner's way of looking at it. Is there no excitement in hiving a swarm of bees, or breaking in a refractory colt? and although the midnight chorus, and perfume of rum are wanting; when we open our windows at early morning during this season of the year, we inhale the fragance of new-mown hay, and hear the blackbird whistle.

What advantages the children of labourers enjoy! They are placed in harness directly they arrive at the age when nature does its best to make them troublesome, not only to themselves but to everybody else, and they are spared the dreadful infliction meeted out to many a young gentleman with nothing on earth to do, and who is "Lord of himself; that heritage of woe." Neither are they torn from home, as I was at the age of eight, and when they are ill they have their mother's care ; whilst when I caught the scarlet something at school, I was shut up in a small attic by myself, in company with hideous night-mares. There were no sisters of mercy in those days, at least I don't remember seeing any. But I remember very well crawling out of bed to get my jacket, and stuff some crusts, which I could not eat, into the pocket, fearing I might be blamed for leaving wholesome food. When the slavey came to tell me I was well, and should have to go back to School, she exclaimed to her companion, " Why, bless the boy, he's got a pocket full of corks."

But those were the tentative days of Marlborough College, when an experiment was being made, how to rear the greatest number of parsons' sons at a minimum of cost.

Then again, the labourer, if he is a good one, can find constant employment in his native village; and is not compelled to go abroad to earn his bread, as I and all my brothers were. In fact, if some scheme can be devised, as I sincerely hope it will, to give the labourer a comfortable old age at home, there will be little left for him to complain about, if only like Virgil's rustic, he can appreciate the blessings and advantages he enjoys.

The best scheme undoubtedly will be one which induces thrift. The Poor-Law gives scant encouragement to that useful virtue now, and if this fact is doubted, listen to a tale of woe.

The only thrifty labourer I ever knew, had such an inextinguishable horror of the workhouse, that during a long life he scraped together out of his wages—which never could have exceeded twelve shillings weekly—one hundred pounds. But when his day was over, and the night was coming on, the Relieving Officer got wind of this unusual hoard of gold, and refused to give him help, either in money or in bread, so long as he could make his savings last, although the spendthrift and the drunkard were being liberally supplied. This appeared of course such hard lines, that he would mount to the very summit of his roof, and loudly proclaim against all idea of thrift, pointing to his own case as an instance of its bad effects, at the same time advising all his hearers to spend every farthing they possessed.

I may also mention among the advantages which the English labourer has, so little does he know about compulsory military service, which all have reason to dislike abroad, that in the hay-field, during the luncheon hour, when I repeated Dibdin's justly celebrated, " All's well," and invited my hearers to explain

> " The sentry walks his lonely round,"

they replied that all must know a sentry is synonymous with *a hundred years*.

The song has reference to the soldier and the sailor, but one of my men who has a poetic turn of mind, requested permission to supply another verse introducing the agricultural labourer. A request with which I readily complied, and received the following, almost impromptu, lines :

> " And on the agricultural ground,
> When snow and frost lie thick around,
> Careless alike of wind and cold,
> The faithful shepherd guards his fold ;
> And as he tends the sheep with care,
> The farmer's voice salutes his ear :
> What-cheer ?   *Joseph quickly tell !
> The cows ?   The colts ?
> Good night !   All's well ! "

This man's father and grandfather were also poetic in their way, and, so tradition runs, they possessed the faculty of " rhyming almost anything." After a fashion, which appears to have been current in old days.

Johnson :   " Sir !   I composed a good line yesterday."
Goldsmith :   " Then, let us have it, and I will add a bad one to it."

* Joseph Shirley, who was acting as my shepherd then.

My man also tells me he can trace his ancestry back in an unbroken line so far as our registers extend, and that his progenitors all lie in our church-yard. So that when I view their last resting place, I feel inclined to say :

" Some mute inglorious Milton there may rest."

But speaking of village amusements, in the summer, none was followed, when I was at home from school, with greater zeal than cray-fishing. This is truly the poor man's recreation ; and on summer evenings the banks of our streams were lined with joyous bands, eagerly engaged in catching the little crustacean in nets. The air till long past midnight was filled with happy sounds and laughter ; and if the hooting owl and foxes calling to their cronies, made the timid keep together, the party seldom broke up without promises to meet again at the river bank to-morrow.

But as I said before, civilization, factories, and gas have completely put an end to this favourite recreation—in one of our streams at least. The sewage refuse and other poisonous compounds, which are emptied into our brook at Chipping Norton, have killed every living thing within it. I and the other riparian owners remonstrated in vain ; and when, as a modern Naboth, I sent in a humble petition that my water might be spared, I was advised to go to law—With a Corporation rich as Crœsus, and lawyers, who although socially the best of men, are so acute in argument that I should be rash indeed to try a fall with them. In fact, justice in such a cause must be viewed like the golden apples in Hera's garden, guarded by the Hesperides.

During the holidays I passed a great deal of my cray-fishing time in company with a farmer, long since dead, who always alluded to any unusual occurrence as " a coincidence which had transpired." He was somewhat inclined to *en-bon-point*, and so was Keren-happuch,* his wife, a very worthy soul. These two one day went to

---

* This, in old days, was a rare village for what were called good scripture names. We had Pharoah, David, Amos, Caleb, Joshua, Eli, Noah, Jonah, besides girls called after the daughters of Job and others.

a neighbouring fair together to sell some cows, whilst their first-born, little Job, who had not yet been weaned, was left behind. But on arrival at the fair, Keren-happuch missed her child on feeling a certain tightness in the chest. Her husband advised her to drive home again in order to find relief: but no! she had come to see her spinster sisters, Jemima and Kezia, and then she strolled away to the outskirts of the town, where soon she found the very thing she wanted—a van, in which was seated a Bohemian lass giving nourishment to her child. A bargain soon was struck, and in almost less than no time, Keren-happuch was comfortably seated in the van, enveloped in the mother's cloak, partly to deceive the brat she now was nursing, and partly to avoid the recognition of any friends who might be wandering by. The real mother thought this interlude a favourable opportunity to execute an errand, but hardly had she passed from sight, when a hurried footstep approached from the other side, and a man entered the van, where silently he raised the cloak, dropped something heavy into the nurse's lap, and then went off as quickly as he came.

My friend with the scripture name, subsequently informed me that she could not make out at first what little game was up; but to her great surprise she found the article, which so unceremoniously had been given into her charge, was no other than her husband's purse crammed full of gold. Just then the mother of the child returned, and after mutual smiles and thanks for favours given, the farmer's wife hastened to the fair, where she soon saw an excited group of people, with her husband in the midst, narrating how he had sold his cows for cash, and how some rascal had subsequently picked his pocket. But of course his lamentations ceased, when his wife appeared upon the scene, and holding up the purse, jocularly asked, whether he had ever seen "anything like that" before.

It may be briefly stated that when the owner of the van subsequently demanded the money from his wife, and she knew nothing of it, he commenced to beat her. Constables appeared upon the

scene, and the whole "coincidence which had transpired" coming
to light, the rogue was lodged for six months in Oxford jail.

About this time, the political economy of Sir Robert Peel, and
Messrs. Cobden and Bright, was the principal topic of conversation
among the farmers. One day I came upon a small landholder,
executing a manœuvre in a ditch : He was springing high into the
air, and bringing his heel viciously down on a clod below. I
asked him what he was about, and he replied, "That's how I would
serve Sir Robert Peel and all his crew, if I only had them here."

Cheap bread certainly was a splendid boon to the generation
which followed the introduction of free corn, but it has left a legacy
of, say ten million mouths, which seem now to puzzle statesmen
how to feed. If anyone wishes clearly to see what ten millions
mean, let him throw down upon the granary floor five sacks of
wheat, which according to calculations I have made, contain about
that quantity of grains. The number seems appalling when applied
to surplus mouths.

Whether the millions which have been nourished on cheap
bread are thankful for their creation and preservation, opinions
perhaps may differ. "Is life worth living?" appears a moot point,
but paradoxically the poor say "Yes," the rich say "No."

For years I have made a point of asking tramps without a home
and friends, if they are happy, and whether they would like to live
their lives over again, just as it has been, with all its hopes and
fears. Their answer is almost invariably "Yes," and when I have
implied that they are lucky fellows, for the rich almost invariably
say "No," they say, "But consider the cares and anxieties the
rich inherit," and I add, "what an unpleasant time many of them
have at school!"

The Caliph Abdul Rahman, mentioned by Gibbon, bore good
testimony to the saying that "Life would be endurable but for
its amusements," when he wrote, "Riches, honours, and power,
and pleasure have waited on my call, nor does any earthly
blessing appear to have been wanting to my felicity, during a

prosperous reign of fifty years. In this situation I have diligently numbered the days of pure and genuine happiness, and they amount to fourteen."

For my part I can fairly say that my happy days have far exceeded the scanty hours of the Spanish Caliph; and although, according to my Marlborough tutor, I had qualified myself for a long period of transportation, I experienced full fourteen happy days after the news arrived that I had passed the examination at the India House, and I was admitted to the East India College at Haileybury. I certainly did not feel the peculiar ecstasy which absorbed me when I heard my father had arrived to take me home for the first holidays of Marlborough College. But still I should have been glad if Joshua could have been present, to postpone *sine die* the progress of the sun; for what I considered riches and honour seemed spread out before me, and I would gladly have surveyed them for ever, in prospective.

Another undoubted evil of unlimited Free-Trade, in this neighbourhood at all events, is that a large proportion of the fields are fertile, not with corn, but with the couch-grass and thistles.

> " *.   .   .   .   non ullus aratro.*
> *Dignus honos, squalent abductis arva colonis.*"

When I was travelling in a certain part of the Ottoman Empire, I passed much fertile land uncultivated, as ours is here, and in answer to enquiries, my dragoman said it was not considered worth anyone's while to cultivate it, for when a good crop appeared the government myrmidons pounced down and bagged it. I think of this when our tax-collector calls on me, and carries off the surplus which my farm has yielded. But I comfort myself by the reflection that I must expect to pay up for the many privileges which a free-born Englishman enjoys, and fortunately I am not dependent on my farm for daily bread. I have kept most careful accounts since I took to

---

* Little encouragement is given to speed the plough. The labourers have left the place, and thistles are rampant in the fields.

farming, and can satisfy my men, and capital fellows they all are, that they receive at least their share, which I acknowledge is not much, of the spoils which my land produces. "But in hope we plough, in hope we sow, in hope we are all led," and I also hope in time, as my land improves, to get a fair return for capital expended.

It would be a happy thing for England if those capitalists who lend money to foreign nations would sink it in land at home, and raise eight or ten quarters to the acre, where now thistles alone are rampant.

But in order thoroughly to appreciate and enjoy a country life and farming, the landlord should be his own bailiff, and work occasionally with his men, for there is no better exercise than to lead half-a-dozen mowers, and listen to the snoring of the scythes as they follow up behind. He must not expect, however, to stick to the work as the labourers do, and I always congratulate myself in being able to leave off when I have had enough hard work. By taking a part in the work myself, I get behind the scenes, and acquire useful knowledge.

Not long ago I took a fancy to dig a well, through eighteen feet of gravel, till I came to a spring of water, clear and pure as crystal. I learnt a fact that time, which sanitary officers would do well to note. I left the mouth of the well open for some days, and when I descended then, I found the water, so pure at first, had become quite putrid, and unfit to drink. But the reason was not far to seek; for during the time it remained open, mice, frogs, beetles and other small deer had tumbled into it, and all except the frogs were drowned. Hence I came to the conclusion that wells, if not properly secured above, are always liable to be polluted. Whereas, although I dug a well on another occasion, close to an old farm yard, I could not find the slightest trace of pollution through the soil itself, a foot below the surface.

I trust I shall never see England divided into small holdings such as I have seen in France. For to say nothing of other evils, the small holders missing their cash on Saturday night would cut

I

down every tree for firing, and then good-bye to the blackbird and the cuckoo, without whose notes the Spring would be a joyless time. I have walked hundreds of miles in France, taking shelter in farm houses when night approached, and I could never see that the farmers or small holders were so well off as our labourers here. They lived on scanty food, and their stores were kept under the bed on which I lay, while, perhaps, a cow would occupy the room below.

"I hope you have slept well," my hostess would enquire.

"I should have slept much better but for that horrid *bête noire* below!"

"Horrid *bête noire!*" my hostess screamed. "Why my beautiful cow has been my lullaby ever since I was a child."

Allotments, where the producer is also the consumer, are of course invaluable to the labourer, but here everyone is so well supplied with land, that surplus stock of potatoes, cabbages, and onions, might be hawked about for a month without finding a purchaser.

I have met in the Riviera any amount of landlords, whom agricultural depression has sent abroad; and when the novelty has worn off, they must find time hang heavily on their hands.

Several of these good fellows asked me one day to accompany them to a bull-fight in Spain; and when we arrived on the scene of action I thought I had never witnessed a grander spectacle. Eight or ten thousand people gaily dressed, seated in tiers around an area quite an acre in extent; a cloudless sky above, and as the carnival was going on, hundreds of masqueraders were performing various antics, of which we had a bird's-eye view. Some bull-fighting followed, to the immense delight of the young men and maidens, old men and children, gathered there; whilst I, although glad to see what the thing was like, should not care to witness such a scene again.

When all was over, and we were coming down the steps outside, a sylph-like Basque maiden, whose face was hidden by a mask, said

A SPANISH BULL-FIGHT.

something to me which I didn't understand, but which, as the crowd was great, I interpreted as a request to preserve her from being crushed or falling down the break-neck stairs, and forthwith she put her arm upon my shoulder until we reached the ground. Then off she went, saying something which no doubt meant thanks for my assistance. By the time I had reached the hotel I had forgotten all about the incident. But it was recalled by an American gentleman, with whom I was acquainted, calling out, " I guess that gal seemed mightily fond of you, sir ! "

" Yes: didn't she ! " I replied, not knowing what else to say.

We were standing before one of those huge mirrors so common in hotels abroad, and raising my eyes, Oh, horror ! a gold pin shaped like an elephant, which was given me in Burmah, and which I valued very much, was gone. Of course, I saw it all ; and involuntarily I upbraided—to use no harsher term—that treacherous maiden, downstairs and upstairs too.

I went to the bureau and informed the landlord about my grievance, and offered a reward if anyone could get my property back, though, of course, I could not identify the supposed robber if I saw her. But the landlord only shrugged his shoulders, and coolly said " he thought I must be mistaken, for the devil never tempted Basques, as he could not learn their language ; and as for the Basque maidens "—here he turned his eyes towards the ceiling —" they were only a little lower than the angels."

" Whatever they may be," I angrily replied, " write up my reckoning, as I shall stop no longer in this den of thieves ;" and I went upstairs to pack my things. But I soon came down again, and at the door of the hotel a breakful of joyful people, who were starting for a pic-nic, kindly asked me as I passed by, to join them, in that free and easy manner so conspicuous abroad.

I needed no second bidding and was clambering up behind, when my host appeared upon the scene all bows and smiles, and seeing me, he offered his congratulations on my good taste in not deserting him for ever, as he was certain sure, throughout the length and

breadth of Europe, I could not possibly be so comfortable elsewhere.   I bowed assent, and told him that although I was not
prepared to endorse all he had said about the Basques, they
certainly were not so bad as I had thought them during my recent
interview with him.   I did not tell him why, just then, as I was
not prepared to enter into a long rigmarole about a slight affair
which could bring no glory to myself.   But the fact was that when
I opened the drawers to pack up my goods, the first thing I saw
was my gold pin, stuck in another tie.

I had no cause for regret in joining this joyous throng, for I made
the acquaintance of a man in whose company, during my stay in the
Riviera, I passed a good deal of my time.   I won't take liberties
with his name, for although I am proud enough of his acquaintance,
he may not be equally so of mine.   I will therefore content myself
with describing him as " a perfect gentleman and first-class fellow,"
the expression used by a French *attachè* to the party who introduced us.   These, so far as I could discover, were the only English
words the *attachè* knew, and he used them indiscriminately to every
Englishman he saw.   But it may be fairly said he sprung no solecism
here, for the name of my new acquaintance with "Professor" added
to it, is mentioned in every seat of learning with applause.

The scene of our pic-nic was on the top of a lovely hill overlooking France and Spain; where the eye can wander over a
hundred square miles of vineyard and olive orchards, backed by the
Pyrenees capped with peaks of snow, which only fade from sight
where the rotundity of the earth dips them below the horizon.   It
is a Paradise for the botanist, though the constant popping of
chasseurs has well-nigh exterminated those rare " British birds,"
whose natural habitat is there in Summer.   Orioles and Hoopoes,
Bee-eaters and Rollers, whose bright plumage, if only spared, would
form a pleasing adjunct to the scenery.

The small-holders in France have also long ago polished off their
fish and game of every kind.   Few people have flogged the Riviera
streams so zealously as I, but I had always to undergo a consider-

able amount of chaff as I hurried along to the river bank, for every one would ask in hilarious tones what I hoped to catch; and when I landed a small trout and spoke of my success, I was supposed to be romancing. But lack of sport in angling could always be compensated in other ways. For life was quite worth living, when seated by the stream I saw Camberwell beauties and painted-ladies come flitting by, or watched the vultures soaring overhead beneath a cloudless sky. One day, as I was whipping a stream with an "orange grouse," a stone came flying from some rocks above into the water by my side, and looking up I saw an evil looking fellow slyly making ready to have another shy. I put down my rod and clambered up the bank to give the man a thrashing—if I could—but when I got near I saw he had a wooden leg, which made me burst out laughing, and I contented myself with menacing him with a stick and driving him away. Some of his countrymen presently came strolling by, and I heard from them the fellow was more or less an idiot, much given to impish tricks.

It always appears strange to me that so few people are able to identify the plants around; and on the occasion of the pic-nic I was holding forth on the splendid flora which this beautiful region enjoys—for it is pleasant to impart knowledge when one can. Here, however, whenever the Professor opened his lips, I had to hold my tongue, and experience the mortification which Goldsmith felt, when a German interrupted him with, "Silence! Silence! Toctor Shonson is going to speak."

We were all reduced to silence, when the Professor, perched on the very summit of the hill with his arms folded, and his eyes screwed up, evidently was preparing for a lecture, whilst everyone gathered round to hear the honied words which should proceed from such a well stored fountain. We had not long to wait, for raising his arm and extending it towards a spur of the Pyrenees, he said, "Wellington drove Soult over the hills we see." Here he paused, looking around to satisfy himself that everyone was listening, and he was about to re-commence when a Britisher, who looked every inch successful, but whose school education, like mine, had evidently been neglected, innocently struck in,

"Dear me! Only fancy, drove over those hills! In a *Diligence,* I suppose ?"

This sage remark reached the Professor's ears; he turned his eyes to mine and gave me a vacant stare, drew in his breath as though he was preparing for a champion dive, and then collapsing on the ground, rolled some distance down the hill, where he clutched a friendly bush, which saved alike further progress and his neck; and in this undignified position he sent forth most awful peals of laughter.

Elia has shown us that a bully is not always a coward; that ill-gotten gains sometimes prosper; and here before us was clearly demonstrated that loud laughter does not necessarily "proclaim a vacant mind."

But as I have again wandered far away from school, I will refer briefly to our village before giving a short account of the stirring events which took place at Marlborough College during the last half-year I passed there. Someone has suggested that I should mention the traditions relating to the witches, cunning men, and apparitions, which in former days put in an appearance here. But to my mind such rubbish is far better buried in oblivion. It resembles the reasons of Antonio's friend, "Two grains of wheat hid in two bushels of chaff, you shall seek all day e're you find them; and when you have them they are not worth the search." The Government did well to brand all persons, pretending to possess occult knowledge, as rogues and vagabonds; for old men and old women have often described to me their fears in childhood when they heard stories—supposed in those days to be strictly true—of witches' midnight frolics, and such-like uncanny things. I would even go a step further, if I could, and brand as rogues and vagabonds all who place in children's hands, books—particularly when they are illustrated—relating to ogres, imps, and dwarfs. Some foolish parents will declare their children love them; but after a good deal of investigation on my part, I find that children, whose minds are saturated with this unholy lore, invariably dread being alone when darkness falls upon the scene; although, not improbably to please a strong-minded mamma or nurse, they *say* they are not afraid.

Every rood of ground which helps to form our village site, if it could only speak, might probably tell of strange events which at one time or another happened there: Those who witnessed these events not improbably imagined that at least an oral record of them would remain until the end of time, as in the case of the sturdy porter who defended the broken bridge at Rome. But my friend, the postman—with whom I often smoke the pipe of peace and friendship, and who knows more about the village in what we call "old days" than anyone else now living—can tell little of what occurred here beyond the early part of the present century. Within this limit, however, we have ample food for entertainment, and even the immortal "Grouse and the gun-room" would, I honestly believe, have to yield before many of my friend's stories as a frequent generator of mirth; and we certainly have laughed at them for more than "twenty years."

One tradition, however, of quite a different type to witches, has been current here so long, that its origin is lost in the mist of ages. It seems to have some connecting link with the Roman camp close by. It has been even said that it formed a favourite theme for Cneius Julius Agricola to make merry over, and that he loved to hear it when, weary with slaughtering ancient Britons, he flung himself upon his couch, or *cubile* of those days. Some scholars, finding words used by Tacitus, have attributed the story to that jerky old historian. But others declare that the Latin is very "Monkish and corrupt." I met with the manuscript in Colonel Barrow's "Log," and on the face of it is written in schoolboy hand, a brief translation, accompanied by rude sketches, which here I reproduce for the benefit of those whose studies have not extended so far as to be able to decipher Latin.

RUSTICUS, JUDÆUS ET PORCULUS.

In rure fragrante, vir rusticus erat, qui in hieme gravissima tristi-que egere cœpit. Nec illi quiddam alimenti ut liberos suos pasceret.

Ad Judæum seniorem, ava-rum-que, deinde üt, et multum supplicans, unam minam pop-oscit. Sed illi avarus, "Pecunia haud facilis est amice ! atsi ar-gento recepto, quale prædium dabis ? "

A Countryman being hard up during a severe winter, applies to a Jew for the loan of a pound. The Jew after remarking that money is " tight," asks what security is offered if those moneys are forthcoming.

The Countryman says he will give a porker as security, on which the Jew is very indignant.

" Formosum porculum dabo ! " respondit rusticus.

Tum ira motus-est avar-us, horrescit, ardentes occu-los intorsit lumine glauco, sic ora resolvit. " Scis rustice ! scis ipse ! ut apud nos porculus vetitus esset. Quo modo bestiam obscenam dare audes ? pudet me tecum colloqui ! Vero ut diceret Cicero. "Quod non opus est, asse carum est." Cito vade rustice !

Dixit autem rusticus, " porculus meus duas minas valeret ! et ego vero unam minam requiro !

Tum ait autem senior intra se. " Quid faciam, ut aliquid lucri extorqueam ? Scio quid faciam ! (clara voce) adducite illum, sed non adducite ad nos. Duc age ad servum meum, Christianum. Ille vero bestiam obscenam accipiet ! "

Dixit ! et nummum exiguum, cum pessima pictura, in manu agricolæ dedit, et gaudens agricola exiit.

Hearing, however, that the porker is worth £2, the Jew tells his customer to take the "unclean beast" to his Christian servant, and advances certain moneys, and an "old master" picture, to make up the full £1. Exit Countryman well satisfied.

In the evening the servant announces the porker's arrival, and says it must be fed. The Jew never thought of that ; but provides cash for food.

Cum sero factum esset, senioris servus, Christianus veniens ait. " Domine, porculus tuus venit, et aliquid dare opportet ut manducaret."

Et non post multos dies, valuit porculus et pinguescit, sicut omnes illum videntes dixere. " Ecce autem, porcum pulchrissimum usitatissimum-que !

In time the animal gets fat, and is pronounced by experts to be a "useful pig," so the Jew tells his servant to sell it at market, as he believes the Countryman will not return to claim his property.

As the servant is starting for the market, the Countryman appears on the scene, tenders the pound and demands his porker, but the Jew in no measured terms demands the moneys spent on food.

His rebus cognitis, senior Judæus palmas suas confricans, in sinu gavisus-est, ad servum suum dixitque. Scio agricolam nunquam venturum ad argentum reddendum. Ad emporium ite, et porcum vende. His jussis auditis profecturus est Christianus. Sed interim rusticus ipse veniens dixit. " Ecce argentum tuum. Da mihi porculum meum senior ! "

Indignatus est senior, respondit-que. "Bestiam tuam pascendo, multas pecunias impendi ! illas restitue etiam !" Sed illi agricola, "patientiam habe. De pascendo in cautionem nihil scriptum est senior. Da mihi porculum meum !"

Verum ubi nulla fugam reperit pellacia, victus dixit avarus, "Me piget stultitiæ meæ. Tolle bestiam obscenam tuam et vade !"

The Countryman points out that there is no stipulation as to food in the bond, and the Jew finding no means of escape returns the pig, which the Countryman drives home.

Tum profectus-est, cum porco suo exultans, rusticus.

Et multa querens, avarus in domo sua revertit.

Whilst the Jew in a state of great indignation and anguish returns to his house.

CHAPTER VIII.

T LENGTH the time arrived when I was to spend my last half-year at school; and when I arrived at Marlborough, in August, 1851, I knew no more of the subjects which formed the curriculum of the school, than I did when I first arrived eight years before; and what otherwise might have been the joyous spring-time of my life had been, with a few bright intervals, little better than a dreary winter of chronic hunger and fear of impending evil in and out of school. No one had ever made the feeblest effort to teach me anything, and the cane had completely failed to drive the Latin grammar into my head. Nor was I alone in this misfortune, for most of the other boys who arrived at school without having been previously "grounded," rowed in exactly the same boat with me.

I can't imagine why the head master did not direct my father to remove me and to try some other school, for all along it was clear I should never be a credit to the place, without a deal more attention than my so-called preceptors felt inclined to give to me. But it was high time that I should make a start, for my uncle, who was a Director of the East India Company, had given me a nomination for the Civil Service in Bengal, and there was clearly no time to lose if I intended to qualify myself for the entrance examination, which would admit me to Haileybury, the East India College of those days.

Although the examination would have been a mere bagatelle to any forward boy; when I read out the subjects to my friends at school they laughed very heartily, and remarked that I might as well attempt to jump over the moon as to "get round" them; and they laughed again when I said I was about to take advantage of a newly-established rule, by which I could have an hour's private tuition from a master in his bedroom, twice a week.

When subsequently I presented myself before Mr. Hutchinson in his garret overlooking the wilderness, this gentleman, who had lately taken first-class University honours, held up his hands in mute astonishment at the small amount I had imbibed at the fountain of knowledge during the past eight years. He raised his hands again when I told him I hoped to pass the best years of my life in India; this time remarking it appeared to him like a longing for an indefinite period of transportation.

We then turned our attention to the subjects for examination. A certain amount of Greek and Latin; the Gospels in Greek; four books of Euclid; Paley's Evidences; Arithmetic, Geography, and English History. In case I omitted to do so at the time, I take this opportunity, after a lapse of more than forty years, to express my gratitude for the patient way in which my tutor listened to my blunders, and the trouble he took, not in attempting to drive me, but to lead me along the road to knowledge. I soon made a certain amount of progress, and now that light was thrown upon the subject, I found that my difficulties in the Latin grammar were chiefly imaginary, and that a world of trouble would have been saved, had I only known that unconsciously I illustrated the three concords or agreements in Latin, almost every time I spoke in English.

Directly my tutor told me that the "Georgics" related to country life, I selected them as my Latin subject for examination; and for those who have never even heard of this beautiful poem, I may briefly mention that when Augustus Cæsar passed his small-holdings Act, giving allotments to his veteran soldiers, nearly two thousand years ago, he, or perhaps Mæcenas, directed Virgil, the Poet Laureate, to describe the pleasures of a country life and demonstrate that true happiness is be derived from the cultivation of corn and vineyards, and in the production of honey.

We may imagine with what delight the veterans, grouped beneath the trees in the Roman suburbs, listened to the poem read aloud; and how they longed for the time when each should sit beneath his own vine and fig tree, where the song of the blackbird, the lark, and the cuckoo should awake them, instead of the unwelcome *reveille;* where the din of battle would be changed to the murmuring cascade, and where the only evidence that such an evil as war exists, would be the rusty weapons and empty helmets turned up by the ploughshare.   We may also imagine, on arriving at the beautiful peroration of the first " Georgic," how many of the veterans bore testimony, with the gesture and circumlocution peculiar to age, and amid the laughter of the sceptics, how they themselves, whilst returning from some revel well lined with Chian wine, had been scared by ghosts, and distinctly heard " the old cow of Mopsus," or " the sheep of Melibœus," lamenting the assassination of Julius Cæsar,

> "   .   .   .   *et simulacra modis pallentia miris*
> *Visa sub obscurum noctis, pecudesque locutæ.*" *

When the fourth " Georgic " appeared, we may imagine what eager enquiries were made for stocks or swarms of bees for sale; whilst the blacksmith, who had been doing a roaring trade in converting swords into sickles, and spears into ploughshares, gave a hearty encore to the lines beginning

> " *Ac veluti lentis Cyclopes fulmina massis,*"

---

* " Pale spectres in the close of night were seen,
   Dumb sheep and oxen spoke."—*Dryden's Translation.*

his brawny arms involuntarily keeping time with the anvil rhythm,

" Gemit impositis incudibus Ætna."

History repeats itself; and lately, when I took the chair at a lecture on Bee-keeping given by the County Council at our National School, in connection with the recent Small Holdings Act; instead of a poem we had magic lantern slides, showing the advantages to be derived from the production of honey on the modern system; and the lecturer threw upon an illuminated sheet the representation of an ideal apiary in Wales, which reminded us of Martin's picture of " The Plains of Heaven," or the home of Pastor Aristaeus in Thessalian Tempe, during its palmy days. Unfortunately, instead of introducing Ceres looking down from heaven with a favourable aspect, as Virgil did, I could only speak of the *series* of bad seasons which now-a-days, both farmers and bee-masters must contend with.

How astonished Julius Cæsar would have been when first he sighted England, or as he sat before his camp fire at night over Pegwell Bay, watching the *Septentriones*; had he been told that his commentaries would be reproduced by tens of thousands; and even after nineteen centuries had passed, form the principal study of little English schoolboys. Horace certainly declared that his works would be more durable than brass; but doubtless it would have pleased him had he been told that quotations from his thoughts would stamp that future variety of his species known as "the English gentleman." And a mirror reflecting what I have written in his honour held up before Virgil's eyes, might not have provoked a frown.

But however that may be; standing as I did, in the rank of backward boys, it was with no small amount of trepidation that I presented myself for three days' examination at the India House. I was not strong in any subject, but classics formed my weakest point. The first day I was invited to translate the 17th chapter of St. Luke from Greek into English; and although a fifth form boy would have rattled it off with only an occasional

K

glance at the book, I scanned the text anxiously before giving
my examiner a specimen of my powers.   But the years I had
attended Chapel at School stood me in good part, for I knew
the English almost by heart, and I was able to advance, though
somewhat tediously.   On arriving at the last verse I felt quite
happy, and was about to give my examiner a homily on the
Natural History of the Holy Land, and how to distinguish eagles
from vultures if he saw them, when, as Natural History was
evidently neither here nor there to him, he preremptorily sent me
to the right-about and called up another lad.

I have robbed many an eagle's and vulture's nest since that
eventful day, and always found the best way to deal with vulture's
eggs was to drill a large round hole and get a low caste fellow, for a
consideration, to shake the contents out.

The next day I was told to construe the peroration of the first
" Georgic," commencing where the poet alludes to the prophetic
nature of the sun.   This was very fortunate, for I know it better
than any other part, and I managed to go ahead, though I felt
considerable relief when I arrived at the last three lines, which
have never been surpassed for beauty or pathos in any language.
Then, after giving a specimen of my knowledge—or rather want of
knowledge—of grammar, I was rising to depart when my examiner
said, " By the bye, what is the perfect of *Audeo ?*" to which I
jauntily replied, " *Audivi.*"   The contortion of that examiner's face
was almost terrible to behold ; he was so steeped in classical lore
that a grammatical error afforded him intense anguish, and I have
often thought my Indian career at that moment was trembling in
the balance.   Luckily I saw my error, and correcting myself, gave
" *Ausus-sum,*" on which his face brightened up and the dark cloud
which had come over it passed away.   I considered this a fine
opportunity for asking so learned a man under what circumstances
such extraordinary things as deponent verbs had crept into the
Latin tongue, and how in the line

　　　" *Agricola, incurvo terram molitus aratro,*"

the last word could be shot down so far from its adjective without the sacrifice of sense? Those were the days of table-turning, and on second thoughts, as the examiner probably would have resented the tables being turned on him, I prudently reserved my questions for a more convenient season, and contentedly retired.

In Homer I had to translate that interesting domestic squabble which ends with

> "Jove on his couch reclined his awful head,
> And Juno slumbered on the golden bed."

Although nearly thirty centuries have passed away since this scene was first depicted by the great epic poet, scholars and school-boys in each succeeding generation of the Arian race spread over Europe, have chuckled at it; the features of even the sternest Dominie relax as he reads how the quarrel ceases on the production of nectar, and he arrives at the two best known lines in Homer.

> "Vulcan with awkward grace his office plies,
> And unextinguished laughter shakes the skies."

I have always thought the Odyssey spoilt the Iliad to a considerable extent, and that it was a mistake to make the heroes afraid of any earthly thing. Who would care to read Ivanhoe again if Sir Walter had made the Black knight hang on to a ram to escape from either man or monster? However, I managed to squeeze through the passage set me to construe, though the examiner doubtless did not require a microscope to see that I was no Greek scholar.

In India I was often called on to play the *rôle* of examiner myself, and I much preferred sitting on his side of the table to the other, particularly when I had to examine the natives in their own language, alongside the English poets; for as happiness, however attained, is the great aim and object of human life, my natural sense of the ridiculous made these examinations a source of considerable enjoyment.

K2

"Now, Baboo," I would ask, "What are the subjects you are taking up ? "

" Mister Shakespeare, Mister Goldsmith, and Bengali."

" Well, sit down, and pray what makes you appear so frightened ? "

" Your Worship, I am a coward, sprung from a race of cowards ; and you appear before me as a lion."

" Oh, if that's all, you have no cause for apprehension, for in the words of Mister Shakespeare, I will 'roar like any sucking dove or nightingale.'   Let me hear you say a few words in Bengali, though I have no doubt you know as much about the language as I do. Indeed, on second thoughts, I will take it for granted that you do, and decline betraying my own ignorance by examining you; We will therefore pass on to Mister Goldsmith."

The Baboo reads :—

> " No surly porter stands in guilty state,
>   To drive imploring famine from the gate."

" What do you understand by a surly porter ? "

" One peevish door-man, your Worship."

" Very good!   See, here is a report from the Inspector of Police: He, says ' he has caught a thief in the act of stealing some rice, and he is sending in the grain to me.'   What does he mean by that ? "

" He is transmitting those corns to your Majesty."

" Ah ! Baboo," I involuntarily exclaim, " I envy your power of acquiring knowledge.   What a good boy they would have thought you at Marlborough College, where your poor examiner acquired little besides the stick."

But this reminds me I am rambling from the point of my discourse, and consequently I will at once return to Marlborough by remarking that what were the causes which led to the so-called Rebellion, which took place during the last half-year I remained at school, those who took a more active part in it could tell probably much better than I can.   But generally speaking, it was due to the total absence of any *entente cordiale* between the masters and the boys.

It is undoubtedly better when possible, to rule by love than fear; but so far as I could see, no attempt of such a method was ever made at Marlborough; and except in the case of a few good boys, who took to learning as naturally as they took to their mothers' milk, it was a constant reign of terror. The masters had gigantic powers, and generally they used them as Fi-fo-fums and Blunder-bores. There was no appeal of any kind, when a preceptor scamped his work in neglecting to shed a kindly light over anything we were supposed to learn, and then punished us for our lack of knowledge. Exceptions there were of course, and judging from the manner in which the few favourites among the masters were regarded by the boys, I have little doubt that both our learning and manners would have made far more progress, had all followed the example of the favourite few.

One of the most reasonable and bravest men I ever knew, when he sent his step-son to school, did so on the condition that he should not be beaten, for he said, " I have commanded a ship for many years without ever having struck a man, and surely you ought to manage a lot of lads without assaulting them."

Flogging has been abolished in the army, and it ought to be abolished at schools, for there is something degrading and cowardly in a grown up man beating a wretched boy for mere want of knowledge, particularly when the assailant himself is utterly unable to distinguish a monocotyledon from a dicotyledon; hemipterous insects from any others; or when invited to discourse about Darwin or Croll on cataclysms, thinking himself now quite in his element, proceeds to explain the mysterious " N." or " M." in the Church Catechism.

" But suppose the boy is a thief or bully ! " some one will exclaim, " How then ? " Well certainly this is a difficult subject to approach, and I am getting out of my depth I own. But I should propose trying gentle measures first, and if it is found that certain convolutions of the brain lead *nolens volens*, the owner to such nefarious acts, I would propose returning the young gentleman to those who produced and reared him, as they probably are most to blame.

A grim smile of deep satisfaction will now steal over the countenance of those who are for the torture system, when they have read thus far. They will lay down the book and piously exclaim, "Here's a pretty fellow; he bags rabbits, purloins fish, runs off with a Tom-cat which he owns did not belong to him, and now he poses as a preacher! What a wicked world we live in!" Well, I confess they have me there; but still I am not going to alter what I have written; because if ever I was certain of anything, I am of this; that had my master called me by my number, or my father by my name, and kindly said, "Look here my lad, I want to ask a favour of you, viz., that you should at once give up, your poaching excursions, and placing yourself and others in danger with your old rusty gun," I would joyously have given a promise to comply with the request, without the slightest fear of ever breaking it.

But we can't conceal the fact that man is more or less a savage animal, and say what one will, two opinions will surely remain regarding the proper way to manage boys.

Fireworks, which were strictly forbidden, having been introduced freely into the school on Guy Fawkes Day, lighted up the insubordination which had long been smouldering. When the masters appeared in the play ground, squibs and crackers shot out noise and fire round them; and one day when the Head-master had taken up a position in the school, in order to overawe the boys, a bottle, filled with gunpowder exploded with a fearful bang in the fireplace before which he was standing, and made him jump as high as I did when the cane descended on my back.

He was fortunately unhurt, though he must have had a narrow escape. I forget whether the perpetrator of this outrage was ever known; but the boy who introduced the fireworks, and got up the subscription for their purchase was discovered, and as he was very popular, his expulsion was made the cause of a monster demonstration. Having learnt somehow the hour of his departure, the whole school, if I remember right, was put in battle-array, and formed up as though in ranks of war. Tramp, tramp, tramp, eight abreast we doubled along the road leading to the town, and woe to any obnoxious person whom we met, and who found no method to escape.

My old antagonist, the Miller, unfortunately for him, was enjoying a morning's outing on his donkey at the time, and sniffing danger in the air, turned round and did his best to fly. I seem to see him now. Bending his body almost double, he stuck his heels into the donkey's sides, working his legs and arms as the winner of the Derby does when he approaches the winning post. But it availed him little, for a dozen stalwart youths flew after him, and dragging him from his seat, rolled him over and over in the gutter; whilst his long eared steed delighted to be free, tore down the road exulting, amid the uproarious laughter of the crowd.

But when the culprit boy came out and entered the carriage which was to end his school days and carry him away, such a shout of disapproval went up, that the Head-master who lived close by, and must have heard it all, doubtless felt that he was quite unfitted to command us.

The Head-master used to wear a garment, which I believe is called a cassock, tied by a sort of *camarband* or scarf around his waist, and this, coupled with his short slim figure, gave him a very effeminate appearance, like some Sheristadars in India.

One evening when I was magistrate of Baraset, in the neighbourhood of Calcutta, as my Sheristadar was sitting by me, the sound of horses' hoofs was heard outside my court; and presently two youthful midshipmen came in and began staring about them in an enquiring manner. At first they only saw the groups of attending natives, but presently their eyes wandered to my chair which was raised on high, and coming near in the cool unconcerned way which sailors have, they enquired if they were right in their conjecture that I was the landlord of an inn. I said their surmise was wrong, but added I would gladly play the part of host if they could wait a little there. So down they sat, and finding they were in a Court of Justice gazed around—at least, so I supposed—with awe and admiration.

My Sheristadar, who had a squeaky voice and wore a cassock, came in for a full share of their regard, though they seemed quite puzzled over him. But at length one of them grew impatient and whispered in my ear, "I didn't know you employed *old women* in the Courts of Justice."

I wonder if those lads are living now and remember the pleasant time we subsequently had together, for I had not seen an European for some time, and was very thankful for their company.

But returning to the School: After the ovation I have described, the big bell rang, and for the first time since I came to School I declined the summons, in company with all the other boys, whilst the bell-ringer, who was an obnoxious fellow and was called "Cock-sparrow," had to beat a retreat and run inside his lodge amid a shower of stones.

Thus the sword of rebellion was drawn and the scabbard thrown away; but although I had no means of knowing what the ruling party thought about it, as I did in the Indian rebellion, which occurred a few years later; I have little doubt that had a vigorous policy been followed, all might have gone off smoothly even then.

A love of mischief comes quite naturally to many boys; and one day, seeing a pair of shoes lying outside a master's bedroom door, some lad injured them so much that their owner demanded the price of another pair. As the culprit was not discovered; a contribution was levied by the master on every boy who slept in the adjoining rooms, and being a good hand at sums, he could calculate to a farthing what each would have to pay. I pleaded abject poverty, but that was no excuse; the necessary coppers had to be obtained somehow, and every morning youths might be seen at the master's desk bringing in instalments. The lessons were consequently neglected, and such a scandal rose, that another master at length was heard to whisper to his mate; "Hold, enough! we have heard, I think, enough about that old shoe."

When the rebellion broke out, this incident was made the subject of unfavourable demonstration; and a leather article which had been discarded from the foot of some labourer or tramp, was hoisted on a pole and stuck over the obnoxious master's desk. But these desks were next the objects for attack; and one day when I was strolling into school, I spied a vandal band going round the place smashing the desks to atoms. It so happened that the master I was under then had never beaten me, and I rather liked him; so I begged the vandals to spare his desk; and I used such convincing arguments on the subject, that they very kindly left it standing, alone amid the general wreck.

Anyone who has seen the comical manner in which a Crane regards its nest when an oologist steals its eggs, may form some idea of the facial workings of each master as he came into school, and saw his usual resting place was gone. My master's face of course was radiant; and hearing what had happened, he, much to my confusion, thanked me in no measured terms, but I, who was quite unaccustomed to such courteous words, and really felt ashamed that so slight an action on my part should be rewarded thus, was quite dumbfounded, and indeed as some kind friends informed me after, I looked exactly like a fool whilst the harangue was going on. They asked me also, why I didn't say something on my part, but I replied, or at least ought to have replied, in the words Dr. Johnson: "No, Sir! when the king had said it, it was so to be. It was not for me to bandy civilities with my sovereign."

What was the grievance of the leader of these vandals, I never knew, or have forgotten; very probably he didn't know himself; but he was expelled soon after, and I met him in Calcutta, as he passed the competitive examination for the civil service, being a very clever lad. His eyes were unusually close together, giving him a sinister look, but he was full of fun, and doubtless full of mischief too. Many a hearty laugh we had over our days at school, but the climate soon proved too much for his constitution, and the last I heard of him was that he had been wandering about in a state of *non compos mentis*, until a friendly hand led him to his bed from which he never rose again.

But all this time dark deeds were being carried on, and I heard some lads had tried to set fire to the school; and whilst chapel was progressing, some of the more daring sprites broke into the masters' rooms, and did much damage.

It was said that they got hold of a manuscript edition of Sophocles, which the Head-master for a long time had been preparing, and committed it to the flames. But considering the numerous editions of the great Attic tragedian already in existence, scholars probably had less cause to deplore its loss than they had when " Diamond ! " little knew that he had committed a similar act of incendiarism.

The Head-master sent for me one day to come into his private room, and there I found him in a state of considerable distress. He said he knew not whom to trust, and he asked me what I thought about it all. But I replied truly, that I took very little interest in the matter, and knew nothing more than what was already known to all. He then remarked that he had no intention of asking me to peach on anyone, for which I thanked him, but without mentioning names, he wished very much to know if skeleton keys were being made use of by the rebels. I was perfectly ignorant of the fact, and indeed, with the exception of the desk affair, I had seen no damage done.

The interview, which made a great impression on me at the time, soon came to an end. When I entered the room I saw one whom hitherto I had regarded almost as a god, but now when I came out, he had henceforth, in my estimation, to take his place with other mortal men.

The old astrologers who saw, or thought they saw, the destinies of men in the movements of the stars, would perhaps have traced some connecting link between me and the first two Head-masters of

BISHOP COTTON,
(The second Head-master of Marlborough College; and subsequently Metropolitan of India).

THE CHAPEL.

THE UPPER SCHOOL.   **STAIRCASE OF THE OLD INN,**

Marlborough College. When I left school the first Head-master's reign there ended, and the only occasion on which I saw the second master, Bishop Cotton, he met his death before my eyes, in the treacherous river Ganges.*

The holidays arrived, the rebellion came to an end, and my school days ended also; but before I had passed the iron railings leading to the town, I stopped to have a last look at the old place where I had grown from a child almost to a man.

The prisoner of Chillon regained his freedom with a sigh; but though no sound like that escaped my lips, the recollections of more than eight long years came crowding in my mind, and as generally is the case when looking back, the dark side of the mirror vanished, and the bright side seemed to turn before me; I was not able however on reflection to deny, that on the whole I had passed an unhappy time at school, and that this was due almost solely to two causes.

First, not having being properly "grounded" before I went to school; and second, Suffering from almost chronic hunger.

I hope I shan't be accused of sounding my own trumpet, when I mention that I found the letter "E." tacked on to my name, when my character for the last time arrived at the Rectory; Undoubtedly so far as looks went, it did very well, for it was better to have begun my school days with "Reprehensible," and finished up with "Exemplary," than to have gone up like a rocket and come down with the stick. But I knew each character was equally undeserved, and when my father demanded an explanation, the only one I could suggest was, that as I had read hungry jurymen invariably give their verdict for the plaintiff in order to save time; so the Marlborough jurymen, who, as I had good reasons to suspect, were kept on short commons like myself, stuck down any letter which came first to hand.

* I gave a brief account of this extraordinary accident in my " Natural History of Monghyr."

A GLIMPSE OF OLD HAILEYBURY.

HAILEYBURY COLLEGE.

CHAPTER IX.

A GLIMPSE OF OLD HAILEYBURY.

N my arrival at the East India College at Haileybury I fell into the ranks of the embryo Bengal administrators who were known as the "Heaven-born." Whether this name was given in sarcasm or not I never cared to ask, for after so many years of qualifying for a prominent position in the Dunciad it sounded very pleasant, and I was content to imagine that it implied superior knowledge not usually meted out to mortals. Accordingly I felt several inches taller than before, and would bring out scraps of Latin—probably misquoted—when I conversed with those who seemed more ignorant than myself, assuming at the same time what appeared to me a grave and thoughtful air.

L

The Professors at the College, who, by the way, were the most shining lights that England could produce, also appear to have suffered from the illusion that we were a cut above the usual run of men, perhaps only a little lower than the angels; for they encompassed sea and land in order to produce the most extraordinary questions, and these they invited us to answer.

I should be curious to know how king Solomon would have got on, had the Queen of Sheba taken a fancy to set such questions at her historical examination at Jerusalem; and I am sure my Marlborough master, who failed to hammer the three concords into me, would have paused in wonder, and thought I must have acquired celestial light somehow, could he have seen me armed with a quire of foolscap and a bundle of pens, sitting down with the following questions on the table, which I was supposed to answer before being qualified for administering justice

> "To the poor Indian, whose untutored mind
> Sees God in clouds and hears him in the wind."

1. Is there any limit theoretically to the length of the shorter leg of a siphon?
2. Find the centre of gravity of a triangle.
3. Distinguish between the geocentric and heliocentric place of a heavenly body.
4. Give the substance of Müller's remarks on the style of Sophocles.
5. Give the laws of the metre in which the Parabasis of Comedy was written.
6. In what manner has Strabo divided the Gymnosophists?
7. Point out any passages in the Tusculan disputations which throw any light on the nature and object of the Eleusinian mysteries.
8. What account has Bishop Butler given of the passion of Resentment as distinct from all the abuses of it, and what conclusion has he drawn from that account?

Instead of acquiring something less than a smattering of such subjects as these, it would have been far better had we all been bundled out to India and placed in harness at once, in order to become familiar with the vernacular.*

But there is no use in crying over spilt milk now. The old East India College, with its attendant nepotism,† shortly after my time came to an end. It had been weighed in the balance and, according to some critics, found wanting ; Civil Service appointments were accordingly thrown open to the public, and all that remained for Canon Melvill, our Principal, when he addressed us on our gala boat-race day, was to express a pathetic hope that the " old boat " would not be beaten by the " new." ‡

Those who were at the head of the Terms at Haileybury, as a rule distinguished themselves in India, so I have nothing to say against the most forward lads being put into the Indian Civil Service now. But so far as my experience goes, much valuable time is spent in studying other subjects, at the expense of the Oriental spoken languages, for some of the cleverest men are painfully weak in the vernacular, and a thorough knowledge of the language of those we are called on to govern, is much more important than the theoretical length of a syphon, or the heliocentric place of a heavenly body.

Unfortunately, the subjects for examination appear to be chosen by those who have not been behind the scenes in India, and who

* Since writing the above, I take the following from the *Daily News* of April 6th :—" The home question of Welsh-speaking judges for Wales seems to shrink into utter insignificance when we hear of the embarrassments of Anglo-Indian judges who are expected to be conversant with the native languages and dialects. Mr. Luttman-Johnson, an Indian judge, observes that if a judge remained in one district all his service he might acquire such a knowledge of the language as would enable him to charge juries efficiently ;" and the Hon. J. Jardine, of the Bombay Court, in *The Asiatic Quarterly*, says, " I suppose every judge finds it no easy task to explain correctly to the jury the definitions, explanations, and exceptions which the Penal Code uses about murder and grievous hurt."

† My uncle, who was a Director of the old East India Company, besides putting me into the Civil Service gave cavalry appointments to my four brothers.
　　Colonel J. C. Lockwood (late 20th Hussars).
　　Captain H. Lockwood (Aide-de-Camp to Lords Elgin, Lawrence and Mayo).
　　Captain R. Lockwood (who died from the effects of an overland journey, in company with
　　　　Colonel Macgregor, through Beloochistan to India.
　　S. D. Lockwood (who subsequently left the Service, and at present is Rector of Kingham).
At one time all five brothers appeared on the Indian Official Register together.

‡ Among the more distinguished rowers in the old boat, when I was in it at Haileybury, I may mention Sir James Gordon, Sir Alfred Lyall, Sir J. B. Lyall, Sir Stewart Bayley, Sir Edward Jenkinson, Sir Aucland Colvin, Sir Charles Bernard, Sir G. D. Pritchard, Sir Charles Grant, Val Prinsep, A.R.A., H. Rivett Carnac, (Hon. Aide-de-Camp to the Queen), J. C. Colvin (the Arrah hero).

consider little can be done in life without an accurate knowledge of
the Greek and Latin grammars, or a facility to extract cube-roots ;
and, even if the question is referred to India, Secretaries, and such-
like purists, dip their fingers deepest in the pie.

I would not allow any lad destined for rule in India, to study
classics or mathematics after leaving school. Mr. Chiswick was a
sensible man, when he declared that the years Warren Hastings had
already wasted over hexameters and pentameters were quite sufficient;
and as for twenty years I was behind the scenes, I would make
knowledge of the vernacular of primary importance.

Land measuring is also a very important subject much neglected.
A district officer should be able to run a Gunter's chain over disputed
land, and tell its area ; and he should be able to tell at a glance the
approximate area of a farm. He should know something about
agriculture, and the crops of India. During "the famine," as I was
walking one day with Sir George Campbell and another high
official, (not living now), we passed a crop of maize, and Sir George
enquired what it was. The high official replied, he did not know,
save that he had seen his servants give something similar to his
cows.

There is such a fearful amount of humbug connected with the
studies of embryo Indian administrators, that at the risk of being
voted insufferably dull, I must write a few more words in illustration
of my theories, for although I am out of the coach myself, I should
feel happy if I could do a good turn for the natives of India, who did
many good turns for me during my time in harness.

I was prospecting Owen's " Anatomy of the Vertebrate Animals,"
one day, and thinking what stiff reading it seemed to be, when one
of my assistants, a competition-walla, (since dead), looking over my
shoulder, said that he knew all the volumes off by heart, as he had
taken them up for examination. Books on botany he also knew by
heart, so he declared, and he presented them to me, with the remark,
that as he had made a theoretical, so I might make a practical, use
of them. He certainly could not identify the beasts, or birds, or

plants around, and when I asked him to visit my museum, he said he hated "Bugs and beetles." But he was a very modest fellow, with all his learning, and would patiently try and make the natives understand what he was driving at, in his broad Irish accent, doubtless wishing all the time, that the hours wasted over Owen had been given to Hindustani.

It is a matter for regret also that the advice of Sir Charles Trevelyan and Sir Monier Williams has not been taken in introducing the Roman character into India, for writing Oriental languages. It is said that no one ever composes good poetry in a foreign tongue, and I am sure no Englishman ever acquired facility in reading the native scrawls. The printed character is bad enough !

My father wrote a fearful fist, and in my school-boy days a story was current in the village, which, on the slightest provocation, was pretty sure to be repeated. That on one occasion he sent some written instructions to his clerk, who failed to read them. The schoolmaster was then called in, as an expert to interpret, but, as he failed also, the bright idea occurred that the manuscript should be submitted to the Rector for explanation. And then came the point of the story, which of course was received with laughter, especially by those who wrote a good round hand. For when the manuscript was returned, the Rector himself could make neither head nor tail of what he had written, look at it which way he would.

But such a manuscript as that, with most of the vowels taken out, would give only a faint idea of a document in India, where all the words and letters

Specimen of fair Hindustani writing, and scrawl, as it generally appears in native documents. In English it means, "Hail cherisher of the poor." Petitions in India usually commence thus.

are jumbled up together without stops, commas, or any such friendly clue to guide us to the place where each sentence commences, or where it ends.

When I read out the Queen's proclamation in Hindustani, before several thousand natives, someone came up and expressed wonder that I could read the Arabic character so fluently. But he ceased to wonder when I showed him my manuscript, which I had carefully prepared beforehand in the Roman character.

Many years before, I had witnessed a painful exhibition which a Foreign Secretary (long since dead) made, in reading out a native document in the presence of the Governor-General and his staff. It made such an impression on me at the time, that I took the hint, and ever after, slyly changed the native hieroglyphics for something easier, when I was called upon to read out a paper to the natives, or in public.

But, returning briefly to the East India College. Some time ago I was invited to send reminiscences of my College life, in order to swell a projected volume on Old Haileybury; but somehow, whenever I began turning over the subject in my mind, I kept involuntarily repeating in the most exasperating way

> " The clock strikes One, supper is done,
> And Sir Carnaby Jenks is full of his fun,
> Singing, jolly companions every one."

The celebrated Bishop of Oxford, who had a hand in abolishing Haileybury, was at the Rectory here one day, during my vacation, and drawing me aside, he asked in a stage whisper, " You are a very fast set at Haileybury, are you not ? "

" My Lord," I replied, " you will never get me to acknowledge that we are *slow*."

But singing was our forte, and the lines

> " *Omnibus hoc vitium est cantoribus inter amicos,*
> *Ut nunquam inducant animum cantare rogati.*" *

* This is a fault common to all singers, that amongst their friends they never are inclined to sing when they are asked. *Smart's Translation of* " *Horace.*"

had no sort of application at College when I was there, for a President had to be appointed at each wine-party, to call upon the guests in turn, and prevent all singing, or rather shouting, together. Our rooms were small, but the numbers who wished to join in the singing were very great, so the College carpenter was called in, with the consent of the professors, to make narrow tables, after the pattern of Evans's, the fashionable music-hall of those days. But even this scheme would not admit every candidate for musical honours, and one stout fellow, who was left in the cold outside, would not hesitate to kick in a lower panel of the door, thrust in his head with half his body, and, whilst on all-fours, join vociferously in the chorus, which of course was intermingled with uproarious laughter at the undignified position of the enthusiast.

When the party ended, as almost everyone rejoiced in the name of Mac something or other, or hailed from Scotland, the culminating "Auld Lang Syne," put every other chorus completely in the shade; for a dozen sons of Anak would raise their legs upon the table, and swing their arms on high in a manner almost fearful to behold. But I could generally hold my own, and make my voice heard above the rest, even in this triumphant song, and though I hailed from England.

My father came and stayed one night at Haileybury. I giving up my room to him, advising at the same time that he should " sport his oak ;" but this he refused to do, being a man of metal. He told me afterwards how much amusement he derived from a stream of tradesmen dropping in, hoping to see me, and get an order for almost any mortal thing of luxury which could be named ; clothes, cigars, scent, anything which was not really wanted ; but their surprise was quite exhilarating to behold, when, instead of finding me at home, they saw a grave and reverend senior, sitting up in bed reading with the aid of spectacles.

Subsequently, when we went round the place, and my father saw carts, traps, and other vehicles waiting at the gates to carry us off to billiards, the boats, Rye House, and other places of amusement ;

and when he saw cups full of cooling and refreshing drinks being handed round to the students, reclining on chairs specially made for ease and comfort, and for holding the wine-cup and fragrant weed; forgetting for a moment his priestly office, he exclaimed, " By Jupiter ! you fellows are acquiring such luxurious habits here, that it is lucky you are going to India, where you can shake the Pagoda-tree."

It was always a matter of some surprise to me that our Professors, with Canon Melvill, the Golden lecturer at their head, winked at our revels; but perhaps with prophetic eyes they foresaw the Mutiny with all its attendant horrors, and said amongst themselves, " Let these poor fellows be merry whilst they can, for even the Aztecs allowed every indulgence to their victims." And the Directors, when they came down in state to see how we were getting on, and we pledged them the wine cup from our windows, also probably interpreted our joyous shouts as

" Morituri te salutant."

And afte rall, the Professors and Directors, supposing my theory is correct, were not far out in their reasons for indulgence, as a large majority of that joyous throng have gone to their long home, and found a last resting place in India, where

" Daily the tides of life, go ebbing and flowing around them,
    Thousands of throbbing hearts, where theirs are at rest and for ever."

I have cut this chapter on old Haileybury very short, as an elaborate Memoir of the College, edited by Sir Monier Williams, is being published by Messrs. Stephen Austin, of Hertford.

PATNA DURING THE MUTINY.

CHAPTER X.

PATNA DURING THE MUTINY.

HEN the "third year" came round, nearly three thousand years ago, we may imagine what an eager crowd of Canaanites and Jews assembled on the Phœnician shore to see the ships unload their cargo of ivory, apes, and peacocks* just arrived from India. What yarns the sailors must have spun about the wonders they had seen, and even "King Solomon, in all his glory," may fairly have waxed impatient to hear the latest news about those mysterious eastern regions beyond the sea.

But since the introduction of the great civilizer—steam, the voyage to India has so often been described, that I have heard not a few declare there is no room for further writing on the subject. As well may it be said that the alphabet has been exhausted, and there is no material to form new words, or that the notes of music have already supplied every possible change of tune; but a facile pen to describe

---

* Since writing the above, it occurs to me that I am out of my depth, for I have no idea where Tarshish is, or was, and although I was among the first to go down the Suez Canal in a steam launch, I forgot it was not open in Solomon's time, and should doubt ships doubling the Cape for the sake of "a whole wilderness of monkeys." Still the servants of Hiram must have gone to India for peacocks, although my old friend Bewick *says* they are common in many parts of Africa.

I should perhaps have hesitated to betray my ignorance here had not my neighbour, Colonel Barrow, a member of the Royal Geographical Society, told me that he can throw no light on the Tarshish question.

the journey in a pleasant novel manner is certainly required, and doubting my capacity in this respect, I will take my readers lightly by the hand; especially as I concur with a great authority in humble life, that the true art of writing consists, not in wearying by prolixity, but in generating a wish for more when the story's ended.

I stepped on board the P. and O. steamer at Southampton with considerable satisfaction; feeling that now I had fairly started, and was about to see something of the world. Every step I took showed something new, and the joyous sound of " Cheery-man, ho! heigho! good gin and brandy, heigho!" with fiddle accompaniment, as the sailors weighed anchor, will never be forgotten. But my exultation cooled down considerably in the Bay of Biscay, where the sea was running mountains high, although the officers declared to me, as their old representatives did to Robinson Crusoe, that it was merely a capfull of wind.

For several days our good ship was tossed about upon the ocean, and I was almost wishing myself back again safe in England, when I fell into a soothing slumber, and slept until the lullaby of the storm had ceased. Then I awoke, and as the ship was no longer rolling, I thought it must be settling down into the depths of the sea, and that I should soon be introduced to the mermaids; so I sprung from my berth, and looked out of the window.

What a splendid sight met my delighted eyes! The steward, who had just come in with coffee, told me we had arrived at Gibraltar; there was the Rock above, and there were boats actually laden with pomegranates, oranges, and grapes, in the clear blue sea below. How on earth I got into my clothes, in my impatience to be off, goodness only knows. But when I did get in them I rushed on deck, and with an ardour which could only have been equalled by Mr. Pickwick, I started off to pay a visit to my poor relations—the Barbary apes, which ever since I could articulate I had heard resided there. That certainly was a joyous day; I was actually "abroad," and I thought as I strutted about how everyone I met must wish to stand in those shoes of mine, and pose, like me, as a true-born Englishman—the incarnation of every virtue. As for the Moors, poor devils, what did they know about the theoretical short legs of syphons, and the heliocentric place of a heavenly body? whilst I had it all by heart. Indeed, by the time I reached India, as my feeling of self-importance seemed to grow at each succeeding port, I probably should have shared the fate of Æsop's inflated frog had not sinister rumours reached our ears that "Jack" Sepoy was beginning to regard himself as equal to his master, and didn't intend submitting to our alleged superiority any longer.

On arriving at Calcutta I was met by the Chief Justice, Sir Arthur Buller, who was an old friend of my people at home, and he took me to his house for dinner. We dined alone, and on the table lay an axe of antiquated shape, such as King Richard may have used in his attack on *Frond-de-Bœuf*, though not so ponderous of course. I took it for a badge of office; but presently Sir Arthur started up, and seizing it, administered many furious blows in the corner of the room, I sitting all the time under the impression that much learning had made him mad. But presently the mystery was solved, for Sir Arthur cried out triumphantly that he had killed one of the numerous musk-rats which, much to his annoyance, had taken up their quarters and held their nightly revels there.

There was a little green parrakeet examining a water-pipe leading from the roof outside the window. "Oh *look*, Sir Arthur!" I exclaimed, "there's your parrot got out of its cage; how will you catch it again?" But he laughed and said, "*My* parrot! that's not *my* parrot, its a wild one; and the rascals, in company with monkeys, infest my garden and do much

INDIAN PARRAKEET.

damage to my peas, although I keep a boy whose sole occupation is to frighten them away."

"But only fancy, peas at Christmas!"

"Ah! that's all very well," my host exclaimed, "you must curb your ecstasy, for the days are coming when you will long for the cool green fields and pleasant pastures of old England."

But after all the years of preparation, all the hours passed with the Latin grammar, wet with tears, lying on my desk before me, and all my songs at College, I was now to be put in harness, and begin some really useful study which would enable me to communicate with the natives over whom I had been called to rule.   To this end the Government sent me off to Patna, four hundred miles up country, and as that was before the railroad days, I went by steamer up the Ganges.

That certainly was a delightful, never-to-be-forgotten voyage; and eagerly I sprang on shore each evening when the anchor dropped to make acquaintance with the strange forms of life and vegetation which thronged the banks.   The old gardener at Daylesford House would show me with much pride tuberoses, which he managed to keep alive, although the thermometer marked ten degrees of frost, and then he would point to a wretched india-rubber plant stuck in an earthen pot.   But here were tuberose trees covered with fragrant blossoms in every garden on New Year's day, and gigantic india-rubber trees with monkeys—real monkeys, not stuffed with straw, as I had previously seen them in museums—peeping among the branches, whilst parrakeets and other gaily-plumaged birds were flying overhead.   Nor was my enjoyment much disturbed by sinister rumours which came to hand about the disaffection of the Sepoys.

After a ten days' journey up the Ganges I duly arrived at Patna, where at that time Mr. William Tayler was the Pro-Consul or Commissioner, holding authority over the city containing 150,000 inhabitants and a large tract of thickly populated and highly fertile country, which in size may be compared to the whole of Ireland.

Shortly after my arrival, as the mutiny was assuming a serious aspect, Mr. Tayler called a Council of the European residents around, and told them in effect that as he dissented from the conciliatory pat-them-on-the-back policy which appeared to be emanating from Calcutta, he proposed, with our concurrence, to adopt a vigorous policy such as, in his opinion, was best suited to the times and the fanatical nature of the inhabitants of Patna. But he reckoned without his host—the host being the Supreme Government at Calcutta—and the commencement of his downfall may be dated from that vigorous address, which we, the "Οι πολλοι," applauded to the echo.

Of course, as we were a mere handful of Europeans, a vigorous policy could not make a very effective show. But the Commissioner determined to make it as effective as he could. We collected our force, such as it was, and armed *cap à pié*, rode through the city each evening, and did everything we could to show the natives that we were a desperate set of fellows, who were not to be attacked without great peril to themselves. Other vigorous steps we took, of course, but it would be tedious to recount them here, and I may refer those who are curious on the subject to Malleson's "History of the Mutiny."

It must not, however, be supposed that I am attempting here to edge myself into the rank of my companions of those days: Ross Mangles, V.C., W. McDonnell, V.C., Col. Rattray, C.B., Alonzo Money, C.B., Wake, C.B., Colvin and Boyle, C.S.I., who, when opportunity occurred, proved themselves heroes. All I pretend to say is, that under Mr. Tayler's orders, we one and all, showed a bold front, doing our best to pose before the natives as a band of desperate men ; and, so far as I can judge, this policy averted danger in my case, and prevented my showing whether I was a man of war or not.

All that time, when the state of the country would admit of letters passing, I was in correspondence with my Marlborough brother, who was A.D.C. to Sir Sydney Cotton, at Peshawur. He had been enjoying very lively times up there. But he thought we were lucky fellows in serving under such go-a-head men as Cotton, and my "master—Tayler." He said the surrounding hills up there had been lined with armed Afghans, who held aloof, watching the course of events, before deciding which side to take. But when they saw the English *vigorous policy*, they came in by thousands, for Nicholson to enlist, and send off to fight for us at Delhi.

I found the volatility, of which my masters complained at school, stood me in good stead at Patna, for, notwithstanding the storm which was going on around, I had arrived at the happiest epoch of my life, with companions fully as joyous and light-hearted as myself.

Another of my companions, whose name calls up many pleasant recollections, was Frank Vincent, the magistrate of Barh, an outlying station, thirty miles from Patna. Ross Mangles, Colvin, and I, whilst the Mutiny was going on, occasionally would drop down the Ganges in a boat to Barh, for duck or snipe shooting, and we were sure to find a hearty welcome. I thought that Frank must feel so very helpless in case of an attack, being the only Englishman in the place, that I volunteered to stay and keep him company; but he took me to his stable, and exhibited a thoroughbred, whose saddle was hung up handy, and he said that as his scouts would give him warning if the enemy approached, he could easily skedaddle, and arrive at Patna within two hours.

Although Frank leisurely rode over to Patna to see us all, when he felt a longing to talk in his mother-tongue; thanks, I believe, to Mr. Tayler's vigorous policy, he never had occasion to try the metal of his steed, except at the local races.

At first I lived at Patna, in a house called Rosy Bower, close to the bazaar, and spent much of my time studying with a Munshi, who, as regards manners, contrasted very pleasantly with most of my Marlborough masters. For he would

"   .   .   .   bend his body,
    If I did carelessly but nod at him."

And whilst at school, my Preceptors would shout out wildly,

"Wrong, of course," even before they heard what I had to say. He was almost too polite, and would declare that everything must necessarily be right, because I said it. He knew a little English, chiefly slang, picked up goodness only knows from whom, but certainly not from me, and he would bring it out so innocently and politely as he bowed and rubbed his hands together, thinking all the time he was "quite Parisian," that I should not have begrudged the small salary he enjoyed, had it been merely in payment for his English.

"What salary did you get at your last place, Munshi?"

"Sir, *that* was too less!"

"But my friends think I shall not pass my examination so soon as you say I shall!"

"Dear Sir, that is all Betty and Martin in my eye."

"I hope it is, but sit down. How is it your patent leather shoes are not so bright as usual?"

"There are many dirts and muds about, my darling Sir!"

But these elegant extracts made me think how ridiculous in my turn I must make myself, when I addressed my tutor in broken Hindustani and Bengali. So I made a compact with him, to which he heartily agreed; that I might laugh as much as I liked at his mistakes, but if he wished to make merry over mine, he would do so at his peril.

This arbitrary compact, unjust and cruel though it perhaps may seem, so far as I could learn was no great hardship, for my tutor never seemed inclined to move a muscle of his face at awful blunders which assuredly would have made a vacant mind explode with laughter. But when he thought I meant to perpetrate a joke, the case was different; for then he would crack his fingers, wriggle in his chair, and laugh out loud, exclaiming, "Too good! too good! aha!"

In a short time he got me through the examination, which, considering the Mutiny going on around, was not perhaps quite so stiff as otherwise it would have been. But my tutor received the news of my success with qualified delight. We had passed many

M

really pleasant hours together, and as he never laughed at my awful blunders, he had never excited my anger or resentment ; so when I paid him off, he bowed and said, " Dear Sir! your friendship reminds me of the ivy and the oak."

After leaving Patna, I corresponded with this amusing man, for whom somehow I had conceived a real regard, until his death, which occurred some years after. He always declared that we should meet again; I hope we may, and I am sure I should not feel ashamed to dress up, as the soldiers say, by the side of my old Munshi, at the great assize.

I have often heard it said that there can be no real friendship between the natives of India and Europeans. But I never took in this doctrine. I am sure I felt very great regard for many of the native gentlemen with whom I was brought in contact. Indeed I can't imagine more genuine friendship than exists between me and my old head clerk, Baboo Troilokonath Lahari, a Kulin, or high-caste Brahmin, with whom I have corresponded ever since I left India, nearly fifteen years ago.*

I was asleep in Rosy Bower alone one night, when an Engineer galloping up to the door, suddenly awoke me by shouting out, " Get up for the town is up, and come to the Commissioner's house, where all the Europeans are rallying, and expecting an attack from three regiments of Sepoys who have mutinied at Dinapoor some eight miles distant." I needed no second bidding, particularly as there was a beam above my head, which would have made a most convenient place for the enemy to string me on, and as my friend galloped off to rouse some others, I made my way to the Commissioner's house, where I found all the Europeans had assembled, fully armed and mustering fairly strong. It was arranged that we should go on the flat roof of the house, in case the Mutineers attacked us, as we could conveniently fire down upon them from there.

* Nor must I forget my esteemed friend, Baboo Ughore Chunder Mokerjee, late head-master of the Monghyr School, from whom, as I write, a long letter has arrived. Speaking of his son, who is now a Magistrate, he says: "Do you remember when this fellow, in a fit of pique ran away from home, and I implored your assistance to find him. You, by way of consolation, replied in words which will always dwell on my memory, ' No fear, but he will come back fast enough when he is hungry.'"

Fifty-eight years had passed since my maternal grand-father, then Judge of Benares, armed only with a spear,* standing at the top of a winding staircase, defended himself and family against two hundred armed men, headed by Vizier Ali, the deposed King of Oude, and for many years after, in the Sacred City, it became a proverb that no one should despair; since the Judge Sahib, single handed, kept a host of armed men, headed by a Prince, at bay.

So my thoughts naturally turned to him, and I selected a spear of similar shape from the Commissioner's museum, and put it handy in case it should be needed. We had sent out scouts, and as they would give us ample warning, we collected the assembled Europeans, male and female, and chosing sides, passed that lovely moon-lit night, playing the suitable game of Hi-spy-hi—for most Euro-peans in India are at the proper age for games—among the orange, pomegranate, and fragrant citron trees which thronged the garden. Indeed, we spent a very happy time, full of joy and mirth. "For they laugh at scars who never felt a wound."

Towards morning, as we were thinking the Sepoys would have arrived had they intended coming, and that ours had perhaps been merely idle fears, some one suddenly cried out, "Hark! I hear the Sepoys coming," and sure enough, we listened to a steady tramp, tramp, tramp. We rushed towards the house, and I nearly fell into the arms of Colonel Rattray at the head of five hundred friendly Sikhs, who had been marching day and night to our assistance. I thought I had never seen such a gallant

* For further particulars of this extraordinary defence, see "Elphinston's History of India." "The Massacre of Benares," "The Story of a Spear" in Frazer. The Spear, of which a representation is given above is about six feet long with three sharp edges. It is preserved as an heir-loom at Hollywood Tower, Gloucestershire. When I was at Benares, I paid a visit to the house, which I believe is still standing, and is, more or less, a show place. My Patna Spear is now in the South Kensington Museum, with the rest of Mr. Tayler's collection.

sight before. Nearly every man stood over six feet high, and their gallant commander over-topped them all.

Then all felt safe, and I took Colonel Rattray to a room to wash off the dust which covered him, stepping over the sleeping forms of women and children collected there upon the floor, and when I asked his opinion of the general position of affairs, he briefly said as I was unbuckling his sword and the revolver round his waist.

" Very fishy! Very fishy! but I think my Sikhs will stand! "

This answer made a considerable impression on me at the time, for although I heard the cannons playing on the retreating Sepoys at Dinapoor, I had only hitherto been in company with civilians. But when a soldier at the head of such a splendid regiment, thought things looked " very fishy," I began to realize some sense of danger.

Whenever I recall the Indian Mutiny, the tall forms of Colonel Rattray and Alonzo Money start up conspicuously before me, for wherever danger was greatest and fire hottest they were certain to be seen giving their orders, coolly as though on parade; and they both possessed the qualification so necessary to a leader, that with them in front, their followers entertained no doubt that they were being led on to victory.

The Commissioner would not let me return to Rosy Bower, so I had a charpoy bedstead put in his verandah, where for several months I slept at night with a revolver under my pillow and my gun lying on the floor close by. I heard the latest news when I awoke each morning, as the Commissioner came into the verandah and told me everything he knew. He also told me all his plans, and I admired very much the confidence he had from the beginning that we should get on all right, and that he would be able to keep the City of Patna quiet.

One morning an Orderly rode up with the news that Major Holmes had been murdered by his men at one of our outlying stations; and truly there was no lack, most days, of news which was qualified to make one's hair come out of curl in times of peace.

SIKH SOLDIER.
(Admi ka Shaitan admi hai).

But we soon got used to it, and took good or bad news just as it came.

The calm confidence felt by the Commissioner communicated itself to all the others, and with Tayler and Rattray at the head of affairs, I felt comfortable enough, and didn't trouble myself much about the Mutiny which was going on around.

One morning, soon after the Sikhs arrived, the Commissioner came and told me that from certain information he had received, he thought it very probable the Wahabees, a fanatical sect of Moslems in the city, would give us trouble and raise the flag of insurrection. So in order to keep them quiet he intended making their head men leave, for the present, their houses in the city, and take up their abode near us, where they would be out of temptation to do us mischief, with the Sikhs to watch them. They also would act as hostages for the good behaviour of their crew.

The arguments used for this proceeding appeared to me so good that I heartily concurred, and next day, when the Wahabee Chiefs arrived by invitation, I received them and bowed them, with all due ceremony into the large room in which we used to dine.

Five or six other Europeans were also present, and after a few unimportant observations about the weather and the crops, at a given signal Colonel Rattray and some Sikhs marched in, and then we informed the Wahabees of our plan for keeping them out of mischief and beyond the reach of calumny, which, so far as I could see, afforded them unqualified delight.

An old fellow who sat next to me was the only one who appeared uneasy, for he looked at me slyly through the corners of his eyes as though he could not clearly understand our little game; but I calmed his fears, and said, " Your Reverence, in your new abode —which, by the way, is much cleaner, larger, and more comfortable than your own—you will enjoy peace with honour whilst these troubled times remain; and you can tell your beads and study the Koran at leisure."

Running my eye over the list of persons present at that historic gathering I find I am the sole survivor, and have to bear the brunt of the charge subsequently brought against us, that this *nolens volens* change of the Wahabees' residence, without any " with your leave," or " by your leave," was an act of *treachery* on our part.

In the insurrection of 1799 at Benares, where, as I have shewn, my grandfather took such a conspicuous part, he was subsequently directed to capture certain Mohammedan nobles known to be concerned in the insurrection, and the historian of that affair records that " Anything like an attempt to allure them into our power by civil invitations was justly spurned, as success itself only renders such treacherous measures, however consonant with Asiatic practice, the more disgraceful."

Men with such sentiments as these enable a handful of Englishmen to hold India.   And no wonder when in after years my grandmother received five volumes of Despatches, the following autograph inscription appeared on the fly-leaf :—

> " A testimony of sincere respect and regard, and also a memorial of attachment, founded on long intimacy, to the honourable and virtuous memory of your deceased husband, from her faithful friend and servant,
>
> " WELLESLEY."

It was accordingly determined at Benares, to plan the seizure of all the Mohammedan nobles by surprise, at the same hour, lest the proceedings against one might alarm and enable the others to escape.

This plan was adopted, and it ended in the nobles being killed, but not before they had killed and wounded several of the force sent against them.

And now for the Patna affair :

Without attempting to shield myself behind the proverbs, " All's fair in love and war," and "Necessity knows no law," or pointing to such precedents as leading the enemy into an ambuscade, masked batteries, or catching mice in traps, or robins under a sieve, there appears to me a vast difference between inviting a man to my house, in order to kill him when he gets there; and inviting him, in order that his followers shall *not kill me,* so long as I keep him handy.

Or, to give an illustration which will be familiar to all. It was surely an act of foul treachery on the part of Jael,* wife of Heber the Kenite, to slay Sisera as she did. But, fearing injury from his host, supposing she had enticed the captain into her tent, and kept him in honourable confinement there, enjoying his milk and butter, until all danger had passed away, who could have blamed her?

Of course, Colonel Rattray and his Sikhs could easily have surprised and captured the Wahabees at their residence in the heart of the city, but a display of this kind was the very thing we wished to avoid, as there was nothing definite against them *then,* save that they were the chiefs

> " Of that saintly murderous brood
>   To carnage and the Koran given,
> Who think through unbelievers' blood
>   Lies their directest path to heaven."

If this apology cannot be accepted according to the strict rules of morality, all I can say is that circumstances alter cases, as the following will show :—

When my Marlborough brother commanded the 20th Hussars, he sent for his head sergeant, who was a pattern of morality and a shining light in every way, and asked him " what sort of fellow is Trooper Jones ? "

" He's a very queer sort of a man ! "

" I hear he intends shooting me at the butts this morning."

" Well, if that is the case," coolly replied the sergeant, " the best way will be to keep an eye on him, and not show any signs of fear."

---

* Deborah, the prophetess, who appears to have judged Israel at that time, goes into raptures over this cruel act of treachery, and composed a very beautiful, and poetical panegyric in praise of Jael. Pity it was not in a better cause. From the little we know about this lady, it is evident she had mistaken her profession, and was more fitted to climb Parnassus, than to sit upon the bench

"But, stop, you have not heard me out; he says if he misses me, he intends to shoot you."

"Then, I trust you will at once put him under arrest, Colonel!" almost roared the sergeant.

Could volumes say more?

The Wahabees had no lack of entertainment, for as their new abode was close to where Ross Mangles lived with me, we turned the surrounding space into a recreation ground, where we challenged the Sikhs to cope with us in feats of agility and strength.

As I had won "the hundred yards" at College, and lately the jumping prize at the Calcutta races, the Sikhs had very little chance so far; but in feats of strength—particularly where peculiar skill was wanted—we found it hard work to hold our own.

The second in command of the grand Sikh Corps, who bore the euphonious name of Hidayat Ali, or the Guide to Heaven, took much interest in our games, and we made great friends with him, for he was a rare specimen of an Oriental soldier; his physique was splendid, and the sight of him, with his sharp drawn sword, running at the head of the Sikhs by the side of Colonel Rattray, was one which the enemy never cared to stay very long to contemplate; and it was fortunate for us that he cast his lot with us.

The last time I saw my friend Hidayat Ali, some years after, he had grown very stout; his breast was covered with decorations, and he was sitting fast asleep in one of the front seats at Government House in Calcutta, whilst a Concert was going on around; but when he awoke he recognised me, and we talked over happy Patna days.

The Wahabees used to sit in the verandah of their house telling their beads, and viewing what doubtless they called our antics unworthy of sober men. But it was quite impossible to judge from their Fagin-like faces, in which low cunning was mingled with ferocity, whether they were pleased or not, for they never laughed or even smiled at incidents which ordinary mortals would consider highly entertaining.

I often longed to know their thoughts, though they might be far from flattering to myself; but this I may fairly say, that whether they liked their changed abode or not, it would have been far better had they stayed there always; for some years after they had to change their residence, as convicts beyond the sea, to a far less delightful place than Patna.

The rural population of the district, so far as I could judge, took no share in the mutinous spirit of the Sepoys, and they gave us hardly any trouble. I was much impressed with this fact later on, when I was sent for two days' journey up the river Gunduc, in order to move all the boats I found from one side of the river to the other, and prevent certain native regiments crossing. On starting, my chief presented me with a copy of "*Vanity Fair*," which I had not read before, and he told me to keep a sharp look out for mutineers. But I soon found that it was best not to trouble my head about the enemy, and so I lay very snug inside the boat reading my book, and taking a stroll only in the evening.

I always found the villagers most polite and humble, and none of them offered to molest me though I was quite alone.

In frigid England, the pastime of swimming gives more pain than pleasure so far as my experience goes, but during my Indian career I passed a considerable portion of my time in water, and every station is careless of expense in erecting a commodious bathing place, where a really happy hour may be passed at morning, noon, or night. Directly the sun had risen, giving light to Patna, we all assembled at the bath, the temperature of which I tested and found to be rather higher, in its normal state, than what is called a hot bath in England. But as the outside air marked an average of eighty degrees, it appeared quite cool to persons swimming in it.

When I was acting as Civil and Sessions Judge of Tipperah, there was a piece of water with a circumference of half-a-mile at the bottom of my garden, and the Magistrate and I almost every day at sunrise having adjusted a slightly buoyant apparatus, and an umbrella to shade our eyes, would lie upon our backs on the surface

of the lake, and allow the breeze to take us where it liked.   The
Jacanas* which abounded there, and lived among the water-lilies,
resented our intrusion with shrill cries, and kites and vultures
circling overhead would turn their eyes towards the unusual sight
which we presented.   The fish of course would fly at our approach,
but there were turtles and snakes which greeted us with a passing
stare, but we did not care for them, as strange to say, although the
sea-snakes are very deadly, the fresh water snakes of India possess
no poison fangs.   I often was reminded of a song I sang at Haileybury, and would chant it out as I floated contentedly along :

> "Strange birds about us sweep,
> Strange things come up to look at us,
> The monsters of the deep."

I often longed to hold my Court out there, and went so far as to
broach the subject to my clerks, who cordially approved, and on very
sultry days, when the thermometer marked over 100° in the verandah,
they would "jog my memory" as they called it, and ask when I
proposed an adjournment to the bath.   But public opinion, and
objections which the High Court at Calcutta probably would have
made, compelled me to adjourn *sine die* this novel and refreshing
scheme.

The time I spent at Patna during the Mutiny, was the most joyous
period of my life.   Hitherto examinations had been a constant
incubus, but although there were still such things impending, both
in languages and law, I had gained experience, and learnt how to
manage them without much difficulty; and, as regards the stick, my
tutors stood most in fear of that.   My companions also formed a
very joyous band, and if we looked serious when bad news arrived

---

* Jerdon places the Jacanas among the Coots and Moorhens.   Blythe at one time was inclined to group
them with the Plovers.   On several occasions when I have stood near a flock of Peewits calling on the ground
(not flying), in one of my low-lying meadows, I could, by shutting my eyes, fancy myself back in my house at
Tipperah, with the Jacanas calling, and I believe this similarity of voice in the two birds has not previously
been noticed.

THE PHEASANT-TAILED JACANA.

from Cawnpoor, Lucknow or Delhi, we soon were bright again, for we realized no danger to ourselves ; putting the utmost faith in Tayler, Col. Rattray and his Sikhs.

We had a Mess, and persons of all denominations joined it, but it was chiefly composed of officers and members of the Civil Service. I managed it with fair success, but it was difficult to please every candidate for food. I told my native clerk to paste complaints into a book, which I have by me now ; and those which appeared worthy of comment, or amusing, my clerk read out in a very solemn manner, and with well-rounded periods, in lieu of sherry and bitters, when we all assembled for dinner in the evening. I select the following specimen, which certainly *primâ facie* appears to militate against my alleged fair management. But the writer, who was much addicted to pig-sticking, riding races, and irregular hours, was prone to see a mountain in a mole-hill :

"DEAR LOCKWOOD,

"The Khansaman (native butler,) declines to give me any breakfast. At six this morning he sent me what he called a 'beefy-steak cut from a pampered ox,' but not wanting food at that unearthly hour, I told my fellow to take it back. He also sent me some beastly toast. Now I do want breakfast at a reasonable hour, he says, acting under your orders, I must pay for two breakfasts. I haven't had one yet ! Is this the boasted English jurisprudence you civilians talk so much about ? These servants of yours are most exasperating fellows, for they give me nothing, though they keep on charging me as though I had everything I want."

At the Mess, every evening, all kinds of projects were started for amusement. Hunting, shooting, athletics, and occasionally we would have a dance—the Lancers being most affected—in which all were obliged to join. We wore no coats, but Garibaldi jackets of gaudy colours, and leather belts, in which our revolvers, hardly ever laid aside, were stuck, and high untanned leather boots, of native make.   These in time were wont to draggle down, giving us the appearance of ruffians on the stage.

Every one was obliged to do what, I believe, are called the steps, and when the fiddle struck up and we all went round, old and young together, those who smoked being armed with churchwarden pipes, which someone had procured somehow, the effect was so very comical, and we looked such awful idiots, that I could hardly stand up for laughing.   Mr. Judge Woodcock, who had been nearly a third of a century in the Civil Service, and who was a great favourite with us all, would try and excuse himself, on the plea of being too old and stout, but his grave face as he hopped round, was far too good to be lost without a struggle, so three or four of us would take him by the arms and compel him to join in the dance, which I feel confident he enjoyed as much as the youngest there.

Sometimes we would hunt the sacred bulls, which roamed about at pleasure, filching the farmers' crops, and as we galloped along-side, we seized their tails and tried to throw them over ; and, once, when some British soldiers were camping near, we ran one in among them ; but they, thinking it was mad, turned out and shot it, the butcher of the party cutting it up for meat.

Ross Mangles and I, however, as guardians of the peace, in no measured terms declaimed against this impious act, and all received our censure in good part, except the smallest of the troop, who, never having heard of sacred bulls before, failed to appreciate the warmth with which we spoke, so, stepping out, he said, " You gentlemen seem to be speaking very disrespectful to the British soldier."   But the comical bantam-cock-like way in which he spoke, caused such a burst of laughter that he was obliged to retire in confusion, whilst his comrades, wishing to make peace, cordially invited us each to take a sirloin.

Our dress whilst the Mutiny was going on around, was most peculiar, but we thought it picturesque ; for when an itinerant native pedler exposed his wares to view, he was sure to have some fancy gaudy stuff, which almost required a pair of green spectacles to examine. "I must have a coat of that!" one of us was pretty sure to cry. "And I!" "and I!" added the others standing by; "and cap and trousers too." The native tailor, who always forms one of the numerous attending suite of slaveys in the East, was then called in, and next morning we appeared in all the colours of the rainbow, much to our own delight and the admiration of the natives. Colonel Mundy, in command of the 19th Regiment at Dinapoor, and who spent a good deal of his time with us, appeared one day in a crimson flannel suit, which made him appear on fire in the distance.

I passed a good deal of my time in company with Colonel Mundy, who in those days had an almost world-wide reputation for his skill at billiards and as a teller of queer stories; but whether these stories were strictly true or not I don't pretend to say. If I remember right, the following was one of them :—

He was shipwrecked. How or where? I quite forget; but he managed to get on a plank or raft, and there for several days was tossed about upon the sea which was running mountains high. A ship approached and hailed him, but in consequence of the tremendous waves it was quite impossible to save him, so the ship flew on and left him to his fate.

Ultimately he must have got to land somehow, though I quite forget the tale just there, for subsequently I saw him alive and well, and he was also able to be present at a fashionable house in London, where, after dinner, a naval captain was telling a terrible story of the sea, which had come under his own experience. During a dreadful storm he had passed a shipwrecked wretch sitting on a plank, the sport of wind and waves.

His hearers, who had held their breath in horror at the tale, gave a deep sigh in unison of sorrow when it ended, and we may judge of their astonishment when one of the party expressed a longing wish to know who the poor man could possibly have been, Colonel Mundy, with much *sang froid* exclaimed, as he tapped his chest,

"Here you see him; I am the very man!" and turning to the

N

captain, he said, "I remember you perfectly, standing on the bridge with a speaking-trumpet in your hand; directly you entered the room I recognised your features. Have a good look at me, and I am sure you will remember mine."

CHAPTER XI.

 HAVE spoken of the country under Mr. Commissioner Tayler's rule, as bearing comparison in size to the whole of Ireland. This was divided into several districts, in each of which there was a Magistrate, half-a-dozen other officials, besides a few European traders, and Indigo planters, scattered all over the country. There were native policemen, but no soldiers in these districts, the only military station being at Dinapoor, on the river Ganges, eight miles from Patna.

The three regiments of Sepoys which made us assemble in such hot haste at the Commissioner's house after their mutiny at Dinapoor, instead of coming to Patna, as everyone expected, went off to the out-lying station of Arrah, where they were kept at bay in the most gallant manner by my friends, Wake, Colvin, Boyle, and other Europeans, who had fortified a house. We naturally thought they would all be massacred, but in case they should be able to hold out for a time, H.M. 10th Regiment was sent to their relief, and Ross Mangles, Wake's cousin, who was living with me, joined the force as a volunteer. I volunteered also, but the Commissioner would not let me go.

Hitherto, all had gone well at Patna.   With the exception of one slight attack on our patroling party, when Dr. Lyell was killed, the city had made no sign of disaffection, and the Commissioner was daily receiving congratulations from all parts of India regarding his successful policy.   Indeed some of us went so far as to address Mrs. Tayler as "My Lady" in anticipation of the decoration we supposed to be in store for her gallant husband.   But here again we were reckoning without our host.

As the general opinion was that the Sepoys would disperse directly they saw our force approaching, when I said good-bye to Ross Mangles, I told him if he found them still alive, to remember me to all the beleaguered garrison,* especially to Colvin, who had been with me in the "old boat" at Haileybury.   But the following day, as I was sitting in my verandah reading with my Munshi, I saw a tall tramp-like figure approaching in the distance, and presently to my great astonishment saw it was Ross Mangles, who briefly said, "We have had an awful licking; the 10th is pretty well annihilated, and I am one of the few come back to tell the tale."

Here was cause for grave reflection, but with characteristic selfishness my thoughts reverted to myself, and I said, "I suppose we shall have the victorious Sepoys down on us now!" to which Mangles said, "Very likely!" and throwing himself on a bed which was handy, he fell asleep, and as I would not allow anyone to disturb him, he slept straight on end for fifteen hours.   He had a very rough time of it during his absence from Patna; having walked fifty miles or so, the last twenty-five under a shower of bullets.   But he had no reason to regret going as a volunteer, because his gallantry on this occasion gained for him one of the three Victoria Crosses awarded to civilians.   My Munshi then retired to spread the news like wild-fire through the town; and I went to the Commissioner, whom I found had also heard of the disaster.   But he, as usual, seemed to take the matter very coolly, although he did not

*For a detailed account of the extraordinary defence of Arrah, see "The Competition-Walla," by the Right Honourable Sir George Trevelyan.

dissent, when by way of opening the conversation, I said, " It seems that we shall have hot work here presently ! "

" But, surely," I continued, " you will call in the out-lying Europeans, and not let them be massacred in detail like the Arrah Garrison. Things appear now, to use Colonel Rattray's expression, so ' very fishy,' that every available man should rally here, and even then we should not be one hundred strong. The Sepoys having nearly annihilated the 10th Regiment, will consider themselves invincible, and ruffians from all the country round will assemble in their thousands, and swell the Sepoy ranks. Discretion is the better part of valour, and even the dauntless Clive under the circumstances surely would call in his men."

But Mr. Tayler said one hope remained. Sir Vincent Eyre, with one hundred and fifty Europeans and two guns, was advancing on the other side from Benares to the relief of Arrah, and if he should be successful all would still go well.

" But if like the 10th, he is not successful, how then ? "*

I don't pretend to say that my oration had any effect whatever on the Commissioner, for he was not a man to ask or take much advice, and I record it merely because I am glad to accept a share of the censure which my Chief subsequently incurred over this affair. But I felt quite glad when he told me he was about to issue orders, commanding or inviting—I forget which, but the point appears immaterial—the Europeans at the outlying stations to come in and rally at Patna.

But if I could have peeped ahead and seen the events which occurred during the next few hours, I would joyously have committed an act of treachery, equal to that which I was supposed to have played on the Wahabees. I would have persuaded the Com-

---

* A shepherd, not mine thank goodness, met me with the remark to-day, that the approaching Winter will certainly be mild, and free from frost and snow.
" What makes you think that ?" I asked.
" What makes me think that ? Why the mouses-holes are all turned towards the North."
" Then I shall have no occasion to bury my swedes ! "
" No ! there is no call to bury no swedes when the mouses have their holes open, as I see them now."
I certainly hope this sage remark may prove correct. But as what is least expected so often comes to pass, I shall cover up my swedes, in case the prophetic mice are wrong.

missioner to entrust his orders of recall to me for delivery, and then, when no one was looking, slyly flung them all into the Ganges.

For the gallant Sir Vincent Eyre, with whom subsequently I became intimate, advanced with his usual intrepidity and skill, followed by his men, who had no intention of turning their backs on the enemy; and the mutineer host, after the cannons had played upon them for a short time, dispersed like a mist before the rising sun, and the heroes shut up in the Arrah house were saved.

Directly I heard of this victory, it seemed to fit in so very nicely with the natural course of events, that I felt quite astonished at my ever having supposed it could be otherwise. It really appeared ridiculous to think that the three thousand Sepoys would stand against one hundred and fifty Englishmen; for although they had shot down the 10th, they must have got it pretty warm themselves; and although they had been drilled by English officers; who was going to lead them against such a veteran as Eyre? In fact, I now felt inclined to say, as Jack Spraggon said to Lord Scamperdale, "There, I *knew* how it would all turn out!"

Jack Spraggon was one of those clever gentlemen who knew exactly what would happen, *after* the event occurred.

The Lieutenant-Governor and Lord Canning at Calcutta, four hundred miles from Patna, when they heard of Eyre's victory and the recall order synchronously, were naturally on all fours with Jack Spraggon and myself—in my later illuminated state—and were astonished how anyone in his senses, could have imagined that things could possibly turn out otherwise than they did. In fact, they could make nothing of it. At last a bright idea occurred. The recall, of course, was *due to panic*; and a man who could perform a treacherous act and subsequently be panic-struck, was clearly not fit to rule over so large a province. Consequently Mr. Tayler was deposed, and Mr. Justice Samuels was sent from Calcutta to reign at Patna in his stead.

But by this time our Patna crisis was over. Eyre had sent the

Dinapoor native regiments to the right-about, troops were daily arriving from Europe, and consequently I placed my spear back into its old place in the museum, and left off sleeping with my revolver under my pillow, where I never found it comfortable.

Mr. Samuels arrived in due time, the Wahabees were brought forward, and as a set-off for the slur placed upon their character, they were at once invited to a conciliatory, let by-gones be by-gones pic-nic, to which I as a free-lance was invited.

If those little rascals, whose tricks subsequently were brought to light, had possessed any sense of the ridiculous, how they would have roared with laughter at all this humbug. But when I found them assembled on the steamer which was to take us on our pleasure trip down the Ganges, they looked as grave in their priestly petticoats, as though a joke was neither here nor there to them.

Directly I arrived however, they one and all gave me a sly look through the corners of their eyes, and although they said nothing, I knew very well that they meant to say, "Aha! my fine fellow, you and your Governor have had your combs pretty closely cut we guess!"

On my way to the pic-nic I met Tayler's right-hand man, a native gentleman, who had given much information about the Wahabees and their secret tricks. Subsequently, when these fellows were all transported, he received rewards from the Government, but now he was left shivering in the cold, and more or less branded with disgrace. I asked him if he also had received an invitation to the pic-nic, but he, in melancholy tones, which made me laugh heartily, said "Alas! dear sir, a new king has arisen here who knows not Joseph."

Although the Sepoys at Arrah had been dispersed, they rallied again in considerable numbers; and this time Colonel Douglas, with two guns and a suitable force, was sent to drive them out of their stronghold at a place called Jugdispoor, and I joined the force as assistant to Mr. Alonzo Money, who went as civil officer and interpreter. His employment was chiefly in getting information from the villagers as to the whereabouts of the rebels; but whenever there was any fighting going on, he always took so prominent a part that everyone exclaimed, " That gentleman has mistaken his profession, he should have been a soldier."

I was in good company then, for Sir W. Champain,* of the Engineers, and I, shared Mr. Money's tent, though I confess I was a mere sleeping partner, as my scanty knowledge of the *patois* of the place prevented my being of any real assistance to my chief. I accordingly spent most of my time in shooting round about the camp, and noticing anything in the shape of birds or plants which seemed either curious or rare.

One day when I extended my excursion farther than usual, I saw in the distance a laden cart, without either attendant man or beast; and on going up to it I found a load of cases filled with wine. I at once set my seal upon it as spoils of war, and when I returned to camp, I told Colonel Douglas and Alonzo Money of my claim. But they said, everyone must share alike. I managed however to get several bottles of champagne for my share, and although we were well supplied, as civilians always are in India, those bottles had a rare manna-in-the-wilderness flavour which was quite refreshing.

Soon after this, Jugdispoor was taken by the troops, and I experienced the peculiar sensation of standing under fire for some time. I think we burnt the place, for the figure of Sir W. Champain rushing about with a lighted torch, now rises up before me, but perhaps I may be mistaken in this particular.

We had a grand batteau in the woods of the rebel chief, Koer Singh; and when the time arrived in early morning for a start, at least a hundred willing hands were present to beat the jungles. Sikhs and Goorkhas, and the villagers who lived around, came forward to see the fun. Plenty of rough music was forthcoming too; drums, and horns, and bells to scare the savage boar or bear, and rouse him from his den. I went forward with the other guns, and soon we had all arranged ourselves behind some bush, or rock, or tree. What a lovely scene it was of joyous freedom. One for

* Sir W. Champain subsequently was Director-General of Telegraphs in Persia.

WANDERING MAGPIE

OR

COOK-LEE

which I had longed for many years, and I would not have changed places with a king upon his throne elsewhere.

A cloudless sky was overhead, and not a leaf was stirring, for the Indian jungles on a calm day seem very still and lonely. The long-tailed Magpie* perhaps may call cook-lee, cook-lee, at intervals, and the distant dreamy crow of the jungle cock may sound a note of challenge, or perhaps the stately tread of wild peafowl as they search for scorpions or centipedes among the grass and stones, may make the hunter cock his ear as he lies concealed, and cause him to whisper, "Hush! what's that?" Eagles and vultures too, which abound in India, are pretty sure to be soaring overhead, and make me remember the tom-tits and robins which I caught in England with feelings of contempt.

But the spasmodic silence is soon broken with a horrible din

"The sixpenny drum and the trumpet of tin,"

besides a hundred men trying who can shout the loudest, in order to stir up every living thing, from a tiger to a bul-bul.

The native hunter squatting by me, and whom I subsequently discovered knew a few English words, touches my elbow and whispers, "*Ham!* Sahib, *Ham!*" and with lightning speed the word was turned over in my head. "The Garden of Delight" which I had been reading in Hindustani, and dictionaries were mentally searched in vain. I could not make out what the fellow meant by "Ham!" But the mystery was quickly solved, as a large wild boar came leisurely trotting up the jungle track leading to where I sat. I bowled him over with my first barrel, but up he jumped again, and went off at a tangent, receiving my second bullet as he fled.

These were the first shots fired, and Colonel Rattray was soon beside me, enquiring what was up, and when I told him, he took the post of danger and followed on our quarry, I bringing up the

---

* Many species of Indian Birds recall very pleasant memories. Amongst them may be mentioned the Cook-lee, which was ever calling in the garden, whilst I was reading with my Munshi. Another bird I loved was the Brown Shrike, whose chatter in October announced a speedy advent of the cool season; as the wild song of the Missel-thrush heralds the coming Spring, and warmer weather, in England.

rear behind. How well I remember his tall, picturesque figure, as leader of the Sikhs. Stepping delicately over the stony ground, appearing like some romantic chief upon the stage, but like a cautious general also, peering into every bush and tuft of jungle, so as to be ready, in case the boar should charge us unawares. This skirmishing went on for fifty yards. The time we took in covering the ground was short, but very exciting whilst it lasted, as this was the first large game I had come across. But when we reached a small open space, among some circling trees, there lay the boar stone-dead, with one bullet through his heart and the other through his brain.

I raised a shrill whoo-hoop, and Ross Mangles came running up, and when he saw the quarry, he turned on me and said, " You're a nice fellow, you are! You must be fined at least six dozen of champagne! Fancy *shooting* such a noble beast * as this ! "

But Colonel Rattray took my part, as he always did, and pointed out the impossibility of riding with a spear, in such a forest ; and, doubtless there were plenty of other boars about.

Although my double shot at the wild boar undoubtedly was pretty fair, I exceeded it shortly afterwards, by sending a bullet through the head of a tiger, at a distance of a hundred yards, as he was rushing towards a crowd of unarmed natives. Even that shot was excelled by my neighbour, Captain Noyes, whose brother " Plum-pudding " I have already mentioned as one of the first arrivals at Marlborough College. This gentleman, who has killed much large game in many parts of the world, saw through his telescope one day

---

* Wild boar hunting, or pig-sticking as it is called in India, is alluded to in the following lines, culled from a well-known song :

> " Then let's away : at break of day,
>   Ride vale and hill-top o'er.
> Scale mountain-side, and stem the tide,
>   To spear the savage boar.
>
>   *   *   *   *   *
>
> 'Mid festal times in other climes
>   We'll think of days so dear,
> And fill the cup, and drain it up,
>   To snaffle, spur, and spear."

When I wrote home from India and told my old aunt that I had been enjoying some "pig-sticking," she, much scandalized, forthwith demanded an explanation from my father.

in India, a huge crocodile basking on a Ganges sandbank. So, in the presence of a cloud of witnesses, he carefully sighted his rifle to nine hundred yards, and taking a more than usually steady aim, pulled the trigger.

Locksley, in his celebrated shot at the willow wand, had to make allowance for the wind; but my neighbour was spared any exasperating calculations in this particular, for the air was very calm; and feeling confidence, as every sportsman should, in his rifle and himself, he set sail up the Ganges, and after a somewhat tedious voyage, found, on his arrival at the sandbank, the crocodile dead, with a bullet through his eye and brain—the only vital part.

But, returning briefly to Patna. As no one had better opportunities than I, of forming an opinion regarding the affairs there, during Mr. Tayler's reign, no one was in a more favourable position for viewing the internecine war—which followed after the Relief of Arrah—between the late Commissioner, backed up by the public voice, on the one hand, and the new Commissioner, Mr. Justice Samuels, on the other; for I was intimate with both parties. I almost lived at Mr. Tayler's house, and I dined frequently with Mr. Samuels, who; so far as I could judge, was an upright English gentleman. He apparently shared the views of the Government at Calcutta, that his predecessor's policy regarding the Wahabees, was wrong, and that the recall of the out-lying stations, was either the result of panic, or culpable want of foresight in not anticipating Eyre's victory.

Although I, for reasons already stated, had no doubt whatever that injustice had been done to Mr. Tayler, I quite failed to see that the orders which emanated from Calcutta were given otherwise than in good faith. Treachery and panic are ugly words, and those accused of such things must expect little sympathy from English statesmen until it can be demonstrated, clearly as a proposition in Euclid, that the accusations are totally devoid of foundation.

We were down on our luck certainly for the present; and I felt we were on all-fours with Mr. Pickwick, when his lawyer addressed him thus : " A jury has decided against you.   Well ; that verdict is wrong : but still they decided as they thought right, and it *is* against you."

Under such circumstances Mr. Tayler's wisest policy would have been to keep quiet, and had he done so, subsequent events, I have little doubt, would have justified his proceedings ; matters would have been smoothed over, and again he would have been deemed fitted for the highest administrative command.

But unfortunately he could not view the matter in this light. Thoroughly satisfied that his policy had been right, and considering himself the saviour of Patna, he thought those who differed from him must be wilfully blind and disingenuous ; and even anyone like myself, whose probity he acknowledged to be above suspicion, if he dared to suggest that possibly there might be two opinions in such a cause, did so at the risk of meeting with a reception similar to that of Gil Blas, when he criticised the Archbishop of Granada's homilies.   He accordingly proclaimed war to the knife, neither giving nor demanding quarter, and as he had a facile pen and pencil,* he hoped soon to right himself and cover his opponents with obloquy and ridicule.

"The late Commissioner of Patna has a good deal of Mister John Bull about him," a native gentleman of high rank said to me, " see what thrusts he gives with his sharp horns."   But it was like Virgil's bull, which contended with the winds,

> " *Arboris obnixus trunco, ventosque lacessit*
> *Ictibus, et sparsa ad pugnam proludit arena.*"

But we must not judge Mr. Tayler too harshly.   Had he been six feet high with shoulders in proportion, he might have smiled merely at the charge of panic, and contented himself with punching the head of anyone who dared to repeat the accusation in his

---

* He was a brother of Frederick Tayler, the artist, and according to some, had equal natural talent.

presence. But he was no bigger than Warren Hastings, and both, like Virgil's bees,

" Ingentes animos angusto in pectore versant." *

Sir Walter Scott says that it is less dangerous to impugn the honour of some men than their horsemanship. But how much more dangerous is it to charge a high-spirited little chap, who, even with the aid of high-heeled boots is little more than five feet high, with want of courage.

Those who explore the Indian jungles will probably meet with a graceful bird, well known to naturalists as *" Gallus bellicosus,"* whose shrill notes of challenge may be heard for miles around. Perched on some mound or hillock to make up for deficient size, woe to any of its species wandering near which dares to impugn its courage. Without a single thought of what the consequence may be, it ruffles its feathers, sets its spurs, and then the hunter, if he keeps concealed, may witness a sanguinary battle, in which, after the first few feints and passes, such fearful wounds are given that the weaker bird is soon lying gasping on its back, whilst the victor, flying to the very summit of a neighbouring hill, sounds its shrill clarion of triumph.

I am sure that if Mr. Tayler were living now, he would not object to such a simile as this, for often with his facile pencil he depicted such a fight. Only, so sanguine was he of ultimate success, that the head of the winning bird bore a marked resemblance to his own ; whilst his rival, with wounded wing or bleeding breast, was lying *hors-de-combat* on the ground.

Those however, who, like the hunter, viewed the combat from afar, required no prophetic eye to see how it all must end, as each succeeding thrust which Mr. Tayler gave, placed the members of the Government deeper in this dilemma :—That even supposing they wished to do him justice, they could not do so without accepting his theory, that his opponents, some of them eminent statesmen,

* "With mighty souls in little bodies prest."—*Dryden's Translation.*

must come down from their pedestals, and take their rank with Machiavelli or Barère.

It may be said, " Well, let them come down from their pedestals if Mr. Tayler was in the right."

" Fiat justitia ruit cœlum ! "

But the fact is, that India is a long way off, and a vigorous policy out there in extraordinary times may be viewed bona-fide in very different lights.

I have always seen many points of resemblance between Mr. Tayler and Warren Hastings, and although perhaps neither would thank me for the comparison, both afford good examples of the varying light in which a vigorous Indian policy in extraordinary times may be viewed. The greatest Englishman of the eighteenth century, considered that the natives of India were justified in raising a temple to Hastings as a demon, whilst the greatest writer of the nineteenth, declares that only one cemetery was worthy to contain his remains; and this writer, posing as " Sir Oracle," has raised his hero, whose reputation was almost sinking into obscurity, on a pedestal which will last as long as the English language.

From very early childhood I had heard of Warren Hastings. My mother told me how he was a frequent visitor at her father's house in Portland Place, and how, perhaps prompted by a natural instinct, he would tie her up by her hair to the furniture or anything coming handy; and when I walked abroad in the village here, old people would describe how they worked for the Governor, at Daylesford, close by, and how he declared as they were building a certain wall, that the thermometer marked two degrees higher than he had ever seen it in Bengal.*   How he would walk for hours together with his hands tightly clasped behind him, backwards and forwards, apparently in deep thought, and how (this of course was a delightful

---

* Either the Governor must have made a mistake, or the instrument clearly was out of order.

story,) he brought home some couch grass,† and told his man to plant it for ornament in his garden.

Although both Hastings and Tayler possessed administrative talents of high order, they both would have saved themselves, and everybody else, a world of trouble had they used honey in the place of gall, for ink, and followed the plan of the Emperor Nang-fu, who destroyed his enemies, by making them his friends.* It is said that Francis, the chief antagonist of Hastings was implacable ; but I don't believe this theory, for in my humble way, I always found, in India, these so-called implacable fellows, the easiest to get on with, if they were only treated fairly, and without a parade of insolent superiority, particularly when one stood a round or so above them on the official ladder, as Hastings did compared with Francis.

In my youthful days I spent much of my time at Daylesford, where, after dinner, my host would read out manuscript verses written by Warren Hastings, in which ridicule of Francis appeared in almost every line. I moved uneasy in my chair whilst the recitation was going on, and like Macaulay, thought my reckoning high ; but the invective was so very cutting, that I was wont to apply it subsequently to my playmates when the evil side of my nature came uppermost, and I wished to "rile" them.

The celebrated legend, "*Mens æqua in arduis,*" attached to the portrait of Hastings in Calcutta, may fairly be translated by the watchword of one of Trollope's characters, "'Tis dogged as does it," for Warren's principal *rôle* in life appears to have been getting

---

† The most troublesome weed we have, and yet, strange to say, I have never found a farmer who could point it out in flower. The creeping root-stock alone being recognised.

* "Hastings had no very high opinion of his coadjutors. They had heard of this, and were disposed to be suspicious and punctilious. When men are in such a state of mind, any trifle is sufficient to give occasion for dispute. The members of the Council expected a salute of twenty-one guns ; Hastings allowed them only seventeen. They landed in ill-humour : the first civilities were exchanged with cold reserve. On the morrow commenced that long quarrel, which, after distracting British India, was renewed in England, and in which all the most eminent statesmen and orators of the age took active part, on one or the other side." (*Macaulay.*)

The coadjutors here mentioned were Francis, Clavering and Monson. A fellow feeling makes us wondrous kind, and Macaulay, who exulted in "dusting varlets' jackets" with his gigantic blue and yellow broom, naturally sympathised with his *anax andron*, who shot Francis, killed Clavering, with an ostentatious display of his "elegant Marian," and lampooned all three of his colleagues as occasion suggested.

Hastings was a dead hand at Latin grammar, but he seems to have profited very little by the well-known example,

"*Parvi sunt foris arma, nisi est consilium domi.*"

which seems to mean, that those who are for ever squabbling amongst themselves, are poor tools for bringing peace and prosperity to India.

into scrapes and adroitly getting out of them again, generally after years of trouble and anxiety which would have been insupportable to mortals less pachydermatous than himself.   His vigorous policy occupied the attention of Parliament more or less for a period of seven years; Mr. Tayler occupied it more or less for one day, and then short work was made of his vigorous policy at Patna, for an astute orator on the other side, like Sergeant Snubbin, led a majority by the nose, and demonstrated to their satisfaction that even if Mr. Tayler had not been guilty of treachery and panic; like Æsop's lambkin, he had been guilty of other crimes and mis-demeanours still more heinous.

Both Hastings and Tayler acted according to their lights; and I have no doubt that to their latest breath they thought the blows they gave were only what their antagonists deserved.   However that may be, they raised enemies amongst men quite as valiant as themselves, and far more powerful, besides forfeiting the "heavenly sympathy" of many thoughtful men; especially those who, having led easy-going citizen lives, had never been tried as they were.

When my Portland Place progenitor, who used his spear so deftly at Benares, retired from the service, he ornamented his spoons and forks with what is called "a crest"; but when he contemplated adding book-plates to his library, he found he wanted a legend to superscribe.   Whilst he was in this dilemma, the Marquis Wellesley called, and hearing the cause of trouble, at once suggested a motto, which was adopted with applause,

> " *Dum spiro, spero !* " *

This motto also was adopted by Mr. Tayler; and to the hour of his death he thought and talked of nothing but the alleged injustice done him, carrying on at the same time a hopeless war with those who had kept him from honour, by refusing to acknowledge him as the Saviour of Patna during the Indian Mutiny.

I am told that three historians of the Indian Mutiny—Kaye, Malleson, and Holmes—have devoted a considerable amount of

---

* "Whilst I live, I hope." As "dog Latin" it may be read, " *Dum spiro, spearo !* " " I defend my life with my spear."

space to Mr. Tayler's case, and that on the whole they applaud his policy. I am glad to hear it; and without going so far as to declare that only one cemetery was worthy to contain his remains, or that the safety of all Bengal was due to Mr. Tayler's vigorous policy—as I have not the face of Janus to see what might have happened had it been otherwise—I will content myself by saying, what after all appears to me of primary importance, that I believe I owe my existence at the present moment to it.

But I have said more than I intended about Patna, and will conclude this chapter by briefly stating that in my time, the Indian Civil Service was the finest in the world for persons of mediocre talents like myself; of course assuming that they liked the country when they got there. But those who conceived an inextinguishable aversion to the mean heat of eighty degrees, the confinement within doors for many months in the year, mosquitoes, cholera, fever, and other attendant evils and discomforts, might well compare their period of service to purgatory. Several of my contemporaries soon after landing threw up the service in disgust, but I suspect they subsequently had reason for repentance.

But whatever objection there may be about the climate, no one can reasonably complain about the natives, for they are the best set of fellows to govern in the world.

Soon after I got to India, I had orders to hang a native policeman for alleged mutiny, and when I arrived on the scene of action, I found myself the only European present. The Civil Surgeon ought to have been there, but I thought it best not to wait for him. When I mounted my man upon the gallows, he appealed to his compatriots around to rescue him. But the sight of my rosy cheeks and awful European hat, had such a terrifying effect upon the crowd, that no one stirred, and when the Surgeon came, the man was dead. I always thought the natives a very tractable, pleasant set of fellows to govern after that.

I arrived in India at a very auspicious time for me, and as it is an ill wind that blows no one any good, the Mutiny and other causes, so thinned the ranks above me, that without any merits whatever of my own, I was thrust into appointments which otherwise I might have waited for through many years, and perhaps never have gained at all. I had hardly passed my examinations, when, as no one else was available, I was sent to officiate as the Chief Magistrate of that sacred city, Gya ; the substantive appointment being worth £3000 a year. Then I was employed for three years in taking up land for public purposes on a very high salary, whilst living in tents; and then I was pitchforked on to the Bench as Civil and Sessions Judge to try a *cause celèbre*, in a manner which made me think that after all there was really some reason for supposing I was " heaven-born."

Only one case of mine, if I remember right, was upset on appeal to the High Court ; but the upset order of that one occupied a whole sheet of the daily papers, and formed a nine day's wonder. It was too long to read right through, but I culled passages here and there, and so far as I could understand them, they seemed to show that my ideas of the fundamental principles of Eternal Justice differed widely from my critic's. But Sir George Campbell, the Lieutenant-Governor, took my part, and the unfavourable comments seemed to do me little harm, for I got promotion a short time after.

Then I was one of the principal Famine Officers in 1876, and when Sir Richard Temple kindly offered me a Commissionership, which would have made me like a little king over a very large tract of country, I conceived an overwhelming desire to see my native land once more.

Just then the men in the " new boat " were crying out and saying that the rowers in the " old boat " were blocking the promotion stream ; so I accepted an offer made to me and my contemporaries, which enabled me to retire before my full period of service had expired, on what I considered advantageous terms. I was comparatively young, my father was still alive, and I was able to settle down under the shadow of my old home, where seated under my own vine and fig-tree, I have been able to realize how true the saying is, that,

"A contented mind affords a continual feast."

A SKETCH OF THE NATURAL HISTORY
OF THE RIVIERA.

CHAPTER XII.

NEW YEAR'S DAY IN THE RIVIERA.

THOSE who have endured a succession of English Winters, and have grown grey without extending their travels beyond the British Isles, must find difficulty in realising the fact that a journey of thirty-six hours from London can carry them to a land where the palm tree flourishes in the open air, where geraniums and roses may be seen covered with flowers by the road-side in December, and where green peas are gathered on Christmas Day. Indeed, were an untravelled Englishman to take a sleeping potion on a tempestuous winter's night, and not awake before he reached Cannes, at a point over-looking the sparkling sea, with the purple heath-covered mountains rising in the back-ground until they end in perpetual snow, he might not unreasonably imagine that he had arrived at those delectable regions described by Bunyan.

But not only are the cloudless skies, the warm sun, and beautiful scenery of the Riviera towns — Cannes, Nice, and Mentone — inducements for migration to escape the English Winter, but as yet the English rough has not penetrated so far, and consequently the surrounding country, with its pine woods, its orange and myrtle groves, are open to all, and the traveller may explore the neighbourhood with a freedom almost unknown at home. To a botanist these shores of the Mediterranean are peculiarly attractive, for not only do many rare English plants make their headquarters here, but of late years numerous other countries, not excepting even the Antipodes, have contributed their most useful and conspicuous plants to add their beauties to those of the indigenous kinds. Here the blue gums of Australia have found a home, and, although planted by the present generation, have become stately trees sixty feet high, with a circumference of ten feet. Apparently they thrive so well that in the distant future, not improbably they will oust the native trees, and look on the country as their own. At present their culture is encouraged so far as possible by man, in consequence of the influence their aromatic juices are supposed to possess over the various ills which human flesh is heir to. Here also flourish the casuarinas, or Australian beefwood trees—those mock conifers, as they may be called, which grow also in my Indian garden, and which are worth cultivating were it only to hear the wind softly sighing upon a summer's evening through their long pendant horse-tail leaves. Several acacias and mimosas from Australia, seen only under glass in England, are also here, and with them the so-called pepper tree (*Schinus molle*), whose racemes of berries, like coral beads, would add grace to the most beautiful garden in the world.

Among the exotic plants which are to be seen in the gardens here, and which testify to the high mean temperature of the air, may be mentioned the bamboo, the date palm, the sugar cane, and American agave, which many of our transatlantic cousins, coming from the north, see for the first time flourishing in hedges here. Indeed, so completely do the thirty-six hours from London change the scene, that on entering the garden of the Beau-Site Hotel at Cannes late in November, it appeared as though we were walking in some gigantic conservatory, whose glass had suddenly been removed by fairy hands.

Steam, the great civilizer here as in England, has long since sounded the death note of stage coaches, and few of the present generation of travellers have seen the beauties of the Corniche road, which runs between Cannes and Mentone, nearly 2000 feet above the sea, and the railroad which winds along the shore. There is no finer road for the pedestrian in Europe. Below lies the blue Mediterranean, and to the north a succession of rocky hills and snow-capped mountains form a picturesque contrast to the olive orchards and stone-pines which adjoin the road.

On New Year's day my daughter and I determined to walk from Nice to Mentone, over the Corniche road, a distance of twenty miles, and make a collection of plants by the way. We breakfasted in the hotel garden under the shade of some orange trees, whose fruit, hanging in hundreds overhead, formed a picturesque contrast to the scarlet arbutus berries close by. The cold morning air was scented by numerous geraniums and heliotrope flowers, amongst which bees and butterflies, and the humming-bird hawk-moth— were breakfasting by our side. Most of the other residents of the hotel were still in bed; but one clerical gentleman, a new arrival from London, was airing his French before the assembled waiters " *J'ai beaucoup de femmes,*"* he exclaimed, rubbing his hands as his breakfast was placed upon the table; translating for our benefit; that the change of air " had made him very hungry." The waiters, however, viewed him with astonishment, and not unnaturally took him for a Mormon or a Turk.

The first portion of our walk lay through the town of Nice, and here we saw the small game of the inhabitants exposed for sale : blackbirds and thrushes, hawfinches, goldfinches, mountain finches, with here and there a woodpecker, Sardinian warbler and jay. These constitute the ortolans of visitors, as short-toed larks and wagtails pass for ortolans in India.

One would imagine that the insignificant size of the gold-crest would have saved it from destruction; but no! here it is exposed for sale as food ; and we saw a stout gentleman come and buy one for a penny.

* I believe this mistake is frequently made.

" You have indeed a *bonne bouche* there," the vendor cried ; " but why not have some more ? " she added, bringing down a string of robins and chaffinches. But on the stout gentleman declaring that he had enough, the vendor seized my daughter's arm, as though a sudden enlightenment had dawned upon her, and screamed, "Aha! he has bought that delicate morsel for his leetle baby."

Here also exposed for sale is a kite, which some fortunate *chasseur* has brought down ; but he must be nearly the last of his race, for the birds are well-nigh exterminated in this country, and no song is heard to break the silence of the woods.

We passed on through the market to buy some fruit to help us on our way ; but although plentiful and cheap, there can be no doubt that the fruit is only second-rate, when compared with that exposed for sale in England. The apples, pears, and oranges would hardly find a market in London, which only accepts the best which the earth affords ; and, after tasting the produce of the vineyards here, we can sympathise with Reynard when he declared that the grapes were sour. The only fruit we largely patronise are the half-dried native figs, twenty for a penny.

By the time our purchases are made the sun has risen high above the horizon in a cloudless sky, and its rays reflected from the sea compel us to shield our heads with our umbrellas, notwithstanding that the shortest day has only lately passed. We were glad to get under the shadow of the castle rock to admire the large yellow Mediterranean stone-crops, growing on the face of the precipice, along with red valerians, beloved by cottage gardeners in England. There is a great want of life upon the sea ; and, although the glossy water is warm and inviting, hardly anyone appears to go upon it either for pleasure or profit ; but as we pass the castle and come again upon the beach, the first fishermen we have seen are dragging their net to shore over the pebbly bottom of the sea. We had not long to wait before a huge octopus appeared, and a bulldog-looking fisher boy rushed down and seized it in his teeth, worrying it until apparently life was extinct, although its suckers convulsively

clutched hold of the basket to which it was consigned. This bulldog-
youth, from whom my
daughter could hardly
take her horror-stricken
eyes, then turned his
attention to the remain-
ing occupants of the net,
which were not numer-
ous or large. There were
six grey mullet, a dozen
or so of sardines, and
four crayfish, represen-
tatives of a motley group
which, unseen by human
eye, must have many a
fierce struggle for exist-
ence beneath the blue waters of the sea.

THE OCTOPUS.

On leaving the sea shore, our road led up among the hills, until
we reached the limestone quarries, which supply the east end of the
town of Nice with stones and lime. Here we sat down to admire
one of the most beautiful views in the world. Below was the Villa-
franca harbour, large enough to hold all the fleets of the world.
The sea was smooth as glass, and where there was no seaweed on
the rocks below, the spots appeared like emeralds set in sapphire.
The town and neighbouring hills looked so still and lifeless that
persons accustomed to the crowded and smoky towns of England,
passing as we did, might think them uninhabited. The only sign
of life around us was a redstart, seeking among the crevices of the
rocks a suitable site for his nest in the coming Spring. Here we
found the creeping asparagus (*A. acutifolius*), the Cineraria maritima,
and the Mediterranean harebell (*Campanula macrorhiza*). Here and
there are stone-pines and cork trees, whose acorns are thickly
strewn around, and whose bark has been partially stripped off to
make floats for fishing nets. I cut an extra stopper for our water-

bottle, but the cork was very inferior in quality, and fit only for making floats or imitation rockwork, such as figures in London window gardens.   Suddenly a loud hoarse cry was heard, and looking up we expected to see a crow fly out, but nothing stirred, although we shook the tree.   Presently we discovered a green tree frog among the branches, calling to his mate below.

After leaving the quarry we scrambled up among the rocks, which were almost hidden by wild rosemary in flower, until we reached the Corniche road, where four roads meet, and where, upon one of the walls of a country inn, an English artist has painted a life-size picture of Massena, who was born at Nice.   This picture at once recalled the lines of Byron :

> " What is the end of fame ?
>   When the original is dust,
>   A name, a *wretched picture*, and worse bust."

As we were criticising this work of art, a troop of girls assembled in front of the inn to enjoy the fresh mountain air, and to perform a dance in honour of their patroness St. Marguerite.   Many of them had good faces; but I am not among those who see much beauty among the peasants either of Italy or France.   An equal number of Bengali girls would put them in the shade.   But, if not beautiful, they at all events seemed happy.   As we watched, two of their number came, and, seizing my daughter's arm, carried her off without resistance to the dance; and, apparently so pleased were they with the result, that they begged I would leave their newly-found pupil with them till my return.   This proposition, however, I was not prepared to accept; so, with many good wishes to help us on our way, we continued our journey.   Soon we found many plants quite new to us in their wild state—the myrtle, juniper, and mountain heath (*Erica arborea*), from whose roots the best briar wood pipes are made.   Where the land is cultivated, pomegranates, loquats—those fragrant Chinese trees beloved by Indian gardeners— and lemons grow; but the recent severe weather, they say, has damaged the lemon harvest in the Riviera to the extent of several million francs. We found a large hornet seated on a lemon looking out for prey ; and, as we walked by the road side among the heath, locusts, looking like small birds, rose up and in their flight reminded us of flying fish, for they appear unable to control their wings, suddenly dropping as though they had been shot. But birds were rare. Here and there a few goldfinches were seen feeding on thistle-down, and a solitary raven, which had escaped the *chasseurs*, who are ever on the watch, was croaking among the rocks.

After a residence in England and India, the scarcity of birds here is very marked. Rooks and wood pigeons are unknown. There are no large trees for rooks to build their nests on, and if there were, a rookery would attract every *chasseur* within one hundred miles, and every bird, young and old, would be killed with the greatest possible despatch.

At twelve o'clock we reached Turbia, which overlooks Monaco, and forms one of the finest views in the world. A gambling train from Nice arrived as we were standing there, and hundreds of persons got out to try their luck at the tables. Many of the English whom we met at the hotels go very regularly and lose their money there. Some believe they can win by watching their opportunity ; but most, whilst acknowledging that they must certainly lose in the long run, declare that they consider themselves amply repaid by the excitement which the tables afford. It is difficult to imagine that a mathematician or an actuary would frequent the tables, for the percentage which the bank will gain may be calculated to a very considerable nicety.

Although I stayed some months at Nice and Mentone, and went almost daily to Monaco, I never felt the smallest inclination to try my luck at the tables, for it seemed like an invitation to play at pitch and toss, on the understanding that I should pay a sovereign when heads turned up, receiving only nineteen shillings for the tails. But I had no objection to sit in a velvet cushioned chair, and listen to the band ; for with my eyes turned up towards the

angelic figures painted on the ceiling, which the music seemed
to animate as the authors of the celestial strains, it only required
a pipe to make one feel quite contented, and exclaim with Moore's
Peri,

"Oh, am I not happy? I am, I am!"

But returning to our walk; A number of idlers from the neighbouring houses came round us as we were enjoying our bird's-eye
view of Monaco, and among them was a youth pointed out as the
genius of the place, who hoped to make his fortune on the stage by
singing. We proposed that he should give us a specimen of his
powers by singing the "Marsellaise." This was greeted by the
bystanders with acclamation, and the youth, who needed no second
bidding, began to sing at the top of his voice, the others joining in
the chorus. Unfortunately, on coming to the second verse, a
donkey, which was grazing unconsciously close by, began to bray,
drowning the singer's voice, and our proceedings were terminated
by a roar of laughter.

From Turbia our downward march began towards Mentone, and
here the successive views of sea, precipices, and olive foliage became
very grand. We shouted to provoke an echo from the rocks, nearly
a thousand feet high on our left. "Who are you?" was repeated
so clearly twice, at intervals of some seconds, that we half expected
to see some mocking ogre issue from the mountain caves; but a
pair of buzzards circling over the highest peaks were the only signs
of life. Here among the rocks, under an olive tree, we found a few
purple anemones, which in the spring will form bright carpets
beneath the trees; near them are pistacia bushes, which are not
molested even by the sheep and goats that browse among the rocks;
their leaves and bright berries are saturated with a resinous juice,
which preserves them from attack. The progenitor of these bushes
has sent its offspring far and wide. Under the Indian sun they have
developed into mango trees, which by cultivation have been made to
yield the finest fruit in the world. The strong turpentine odour of

the leaves of both these distant cousins, as they may be called, is still undistinguishable. Here also by the road side we saw the far-famed Carob tree, which has lately flowered and bears its young

THE CAROB BEAN.

horse beans thick upon its branches.   This abnormal member of the great pea family has so far advanced in the scale of excellence as to bear its male and female flowers on separate trees ; and the student of botany, after reading a diagnosis of the order as usually set forth in manuals, must feel sorely puzzled when he sees this tree. Packets of Carob seeds were distributed by the Indian Government some years ago, but I have not heard whether the experiment of introducing the tree into India has succeeded.

We now arrived at a corner of the road from which the town of Mentone appeared a thousand feet below us, with Italy beyond. A stream of pure cold water issued from the rock above, and some benevolent person has placed a drinking fountain there, where thirsty travellers can drink. May his shadow never grow less! and many men and beasts must gratefully have slaked their thirst, as we did, there. The birds even have reason to be grateful, for we saw a robin sitting by the water as we approached, but instinctively he hurried off, fearing we should kill him for the pot. Above our heads, on a thirsty-looking rock, we saw the beautiful sea lavatera in flower, side by side with the Mediterranean sarsaparilla (*Smilax aspera*), whose red berries remind one of the bryony of English hedgerows. Here also are the head-quarters of the wild carrot, which appears in every field, disputing each inch of ground with the purple cuckoo-pint, whose poisonous look reminds one of the Indian cobra with hood erect.

Up to the point where the branch road from Mentone to Monaco joins the Corniche road, a distance of sixteen miles from Nice, we met no one, but now many carriages came in view, the horses, generally galloping, carrying persons who appeared in desperate haste to lose their money at the tables. A well-appointed carriage with four horses and postillions, also passed, and as we watched it turning a sharp corner, one of the wheels caught against a projecting rock and threw the carriage upon its side. On running up we learnt that this was the property of the Prince of Monaco, going to meet him at the station. Although very little damage was done, the box-seat was overhanging a deep precipice, and had anyone been sitting there when the collision occurred, he must have been shot out and fallen sixty feet into the ravine below.

It was now past noon, and the sun was very hot. We had

collected as many plants on the road as we could carry, and were glad to see the plane trees, forming at this season a leafless avenue leading into Mentone, which town we reached at two p.m., having enjoyed one of the most beautiful and pleasant walks that we have taken in our lives. We felt only one regret, that our friends in ice-bound England were not with us to share our pleasure.

CHAPTER XIII.

SPRING IN THE RIVIERA.

EW parts of the earth are so rich in wild flowers as the country round Mentone, known as "*Les Alpes Maritimes.*" The land, where cultivation is possible, has been dug over from a time when the Druids ruled in Britain; and every step taken beneath the olive trees is on ground

"Where once a garden smiled,
And now where many a garden flower grows wild—"

Tulips and lilies, myrtles and orchids and anemones, whose stamens, through generations of high feeding, have become converted into brilliant-coloured petals. The variety of the plants is quite as remarkable as their colour. The great pea family has four times as many representative species in "*Les Alpes Maritimes*" as are to be found in the British Isles; and the vast plains of Bengal probably do not contain one-half the number of plants which a resident of

Mentone may find within a single day's journey from his home. Then the Labiates have twice as many species as are included in the British flora ; and the Composites, which threaten in time to drive all other competitors into the sea, outnumber their cousins across the channel by nearly two hundred species.

But, whilst so much may be said in favour of the flora of Mentone —for neither India, Burmah, nor Brazil can produce more beautiful bouquets of wild flowers—the absence of stately trees and dense foliage is remarkable throughout the Riviera. The only deciduous trees of any size to be seen, are an elm tree at Gorbio—planted, so an inscription says, in 1711—and here and there a few Spanish chestnuts, which would only rank as second-class trees in England. Hence the scarcity of birds along the Mediterranean shores, for they cannot escape the prying eyes of *chasseurs*, who are ever on the watch to kill them, great and small, as lawful game. The pines and olives, the orange and lemon trees and vineyards which cover the country, afford also indifferent shelter for nests, and, after exploring the hills for miles, it is difficult to find a hedgerow or thicket where even a thrush would care to lay her eggs. Rooks and wood-pigeons are unknown, and only occasionally a pair of ravens may be seen circling over some tremendous precipice, where their young ones can be reared in safety. In Spring, before the so-called sportsmen have found them out, birds rarely seen in England occasionally appear, and delight the eyes of naturalists who visit the Riviera. The beautiful and very conspicuous wood-chat shrike lingered for some days in an orchard attached to my villa at Pau, and on several occasions I saw the hoopoe and golden oriole in the neighbourhood.

But, notwithstanding the scarcity of birds, the naturalist who passes the Winter at Mentone need not find the time pass heavy on his hands. The geologist may examine a hundred miles of quarry along the Corniche road, hewn out of the solid rock. The palæon-tologist may speculate on the bones and flints found in the limestone caves close to the town. The entomologist may chase swallow-tails, painted ladies, and Camberwell beauties, over sunny hills and valleys; and whilst the arachnologist is studying the domestic economy of the trapdoor spiders found in every mossy bank, he who takes an interest in the inhabitants of the sea will find an endless variety in the fishermen's nets, or exposed for sale daily in the markets.

There is probably no road in Europe which offers so many attractions to the naturalist or pedestrian as that which runs between Nice and Genoa. As its name—"Corniche"—implies, it is cut on the side of the mountains which rise out of the Mediterranean, and during its entire length of a hundred and thirty miles the sea breaks upon the rocks below, whilst a succession of hills, valleys, gorges, pine forests, and peeps of distant snow succeed each other in endless variety. But the road is now almost deserted for the line of rail, which passes along the shore through at least a hundred tunnels, so that the most beautiful points of the road are passed by the railway travellers unseen.

On New Year's Day I walked from Nice to Mentone, the first part of the Corniche road, and even then the surrounding country was green and beautiful; but when the Spring arrived, and wild flowers were everywhere starting into life, I determined to continue my walk to Genoa.

Soon after sunrise my companion, Mr. Holcroft, and I set out. The sky, as usual in Mentone, was cloudless, and the only sounds which disturbed the morning air were the murmur of the waves of the Mediterranean breaking on the pebbly beach, and the chorus of a thousand green frogs perched up in the branches of the surrounding orange groves. We paused for a few moments under a neem tree (*Melia*) to watch the Corsican mountains eighty miles distant, and the scene recalled a time in India when, standing under a similar tree in my garden, I watched Mount Everest, the highest mountain in the world, from a distance of one hundred and eighty miles. But here the panorama soon faded from our view before the rising sun, and we then passed on to the market, where at that early

VIEW ON THE ROAD TO GENOA.

hour baskets of octopi were coming in, together with sea urchins and sea wolves (*loup*), millions of small fry—which are eaten raw—snails and thrushes, to feed the people of the town. The women who kept the stalls were glad to see me, for I often paid them a visit, and would purchase for a trifle what no one else would buy—fishing frogs and sting-fish, spider-crabs and mantis shrimps, just arrived from the bottom of the sea. The basket which I carried was soon filled with sufficient specimens to stock a good-sized aquarium, and as I moved away more than one epicure would exclaim, "*Chacun à son gout.*" But the morning of our walk we could not remain to purchase, and we went on through the Eastern Bay, over whose deep blue waves the sun was throwing a flood of light, reflecting near the shore the caves in the red rocks which mark the boundary line of Italy, and which in ages past formed the picturesque habitation of primeval man, whose records, after lying hidden in the earth for ages, are now being dug up and read. We thought as we stood below the caves, that if the rocks could only speak and tell us what had passed before them, how full of interest the history would be. Were men always either making love or fighting then, as they are now? Were these palatial caves won and kept without a struggle? And if, as probably was the case, many a fierce struggle took place on their account, were the vanquished thrown over the rocks into the sea below us; or were they eaten? Then how did the innumerable bones of lions, bears, and deer and horses become mingled with the dust within the caves? And what was the history of the men whose skeletons were found lately, nineteen feet below the soil? As we thought about these things, and my companion was soliloquising about the evolution of man and the speedy advent of the Millennium, we scrambled up into the smallest cave, which had hitherto been very little disturbed, and, on entering it were astonished to find a man destitute of clothing, *in puris naturalibus*, lying basking in the sun, breakfasting on limpets which he had caught on the rocks below. This original picture of primeval-like man in a primeval cave was not of long duration, for the fellow, who appeared equally surprised as we were, jumped up, and retreating to the further end of the cavern, hastily put on his clothes, and, running down the bank, joined some navvies, his companions, who were working on the railroad below us—leaving us to our own reflections regarding the evolution of man and the Millennium.

These caves are well known to science.   Two of them have been cleared out, and their contents duly recorded in works relating to pre-historic man.   The smaller cave in which we stood has several feet of soil almost undisturbed, and any visitor to Mentone, with a few pounds to spare, might probably get leave to amuse himself next Winter by clearing out the earth and collecting the bones and flints and other treasures which lie buried there.   We contented ourselves by taking some flint chippings and a bone needle as mementoes of our visit, and, scrambling down the bank again, we passed on to a quarry by the road side, where the workmen have lately opened out another cave, and where heaps of bones lie scattered about the place.

The old ganger, who has learnt the value of the relics found within the caves, has many of these things for sale, and, as he has picked up some information about them from the *savants* who have been there, like Captain Cuttle in charge of the scientific instrument maker's shop, he sets himself up as a man of science, and retails his information to anyone who will listen.   He begins with assuring his hearers that his wares are of "*grande antiquité*," words he delights to linger over and repeat ; then, taking a pointed flint, he bares his arm and demonstrates how the primeval doctor used it as a lancet. Then taking some red ochre and some charcoal found within the cave, he smears a little on his face, to show that the cave dwellers adorned themselves and were partial to *rouge et noir*, as their descendants are at Monte Carlo now.   The nummulites, found by thousands in the rocks, he describes as the money of those days, and then with great mystery he pulls out his tobacco-box, and, holding up a human tooth found many yards below the soil, he declares it to be a *dent de Chrétien.*   He invited us to buy, but I pleaded being only a poor *savant* like himself, adding that if he could spare any of

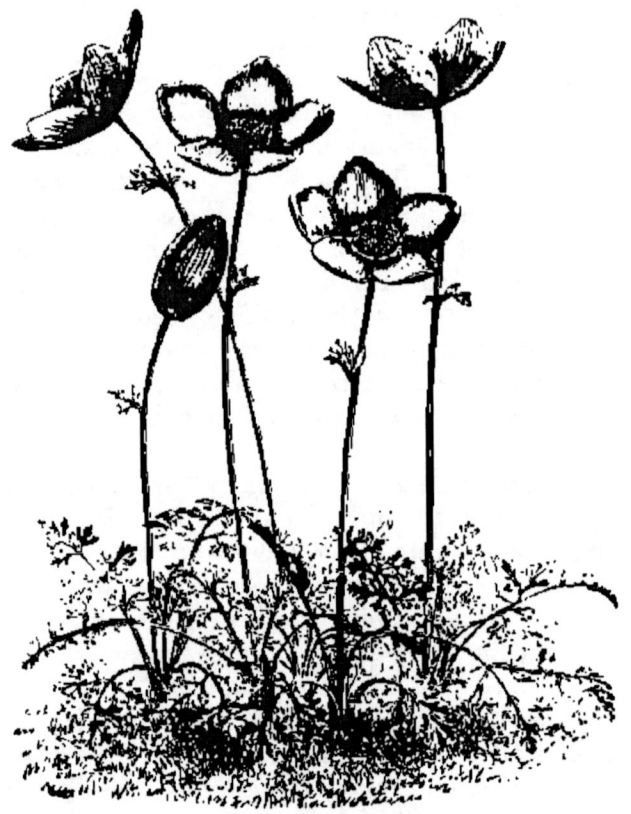

THE ANEMONE.

his treasures for so small a sum as ten centimes as a memento of his lecture, that coin was at his disposal.

It was worth that sum to see the struggle which ensued between

Q

the thrift, for which the inhabitants of these shores are noted, and the anxiety to deal fairly with one who had proclaimed himself a poor man of science like himself. It reminded us of the scene in " Ivanhoe " where Gurth is paying Isaac for his master's armour. But in this instance generosity prevailed ; for, after running his trembling fingers for some time over his treasures, the old man at last pounced down, as an equivalent for my coin, on a fossil bivalve worth at least three-halfpence.

By this time the sun was high above the horizon, and we had only come two miles ; so we wished our entertainer good-bye and the speedy disposal of his wares. The rocks around are celebrated not only for their caves, but also for a deep and picturesque gorge, where a stream of water comes tumbling down a precipice fully five hundred feet high ; an ancient aqueduct with arches spans the rocks within ; whilst high up, suspended in mid-air, is a limestone bridge which separates France from Italy. Here many plants have found a home. The mauve Lavatera, which, like most of the mallow family, has conspicuous flowers, is common there ; and by its side are gorse-like coronilla bushes, bright with crowds of yellow blossoms. Wild thyme is also there, and rosemary, beloved by bees, whilst maiden-hair ferns grow in great profusion by the water-side. Many butterflies select this spot, for high mountains shelter it on the north, and the bright sun, reflected from the rocks, keeps perpetual summer there. Our road led us through olive gardens, and terraces of lemon trees, whose golden fruit lay scattered in hundreds on the ground. Orange groves were also passed ; but the mere thought of a Mentone orange sets one's teeth on edge, and the people of the Riviera, who adore Columbus, have great cause for gratitude in his finding a country where they can dispose of their inferior fruit for flavouring gin-slings and cocktails.

The fourth milestone brought us to Mr. Hanbury's celebrated garden, which during this Anemone season is at its best. The garden stands some three hundred feet above the sea. On one side are yellow and red rocks, with distant purple hills ; below, bordering on the sea, are emerald-coloured pines and bushes of yellow spurge, which in the dazzling sun appear like huge topazes set in among the rocks; whilst the distant white town of Bordighera, at the extremity of an undulating promontory, resembles the ivory horn of some huge

THE TUNNY FISH.

monster thrust into the sea. Within the gardens are the choicest plants, collected from every country which has a climate like Mentone—blue-gum trees, acacias and minosas, palms and aloes, with lilies and roses of every shade and hue. But the chief attraction are the Anemones, thousands of which were growing side by side, with brilliant-coloured tulips, producing a panorama never to be forgotten. A thrush in an orange tree was trying to drown the distant murmur of the waves, and the sighing of the wind through the horsetail leaves of the casuarina trees produced a mysterious dreamy feeling which made my companion subsequently, not without reason, exclaim, " I have been in heaven." But there is only one step from the sublime to the ridiculous. An old lady with two daughters was also visiting the garden, and in no measured terms she was instructing them in botany. " Here you see," she cried, " my dears, is the aloe, which flourishes once only in a hundred years. There," pointing to the eucalyptus tree, " you have the gum tree, from which our gum arabic is made; and there," directing their attention to a casuarina tree, " you see the asparagus of Australia."

The day hitherto had been beautiful and clear; but now the clouds which had been gathering over the mountain-tops were spreading out towards the sea, and a cold wind swept down the valley, raising clouds of dust. By the time we reached Bordighera the sea was white with foam, and we witnessed one of those mimic tempests which have blown over many a sail, and which cost the life of Shelley.

At the neighbouring headland some men were erecting a platform near the sea, in order to watch for Tunnies, those huge fish whose migration from the Atlantic Ocean into the warm waters of the Mediterranean is as regular now as it was 2000 years ago. This may have been the very spot where the love-sick swain mentioned by Theocritus is supposed to have intended hurling himself:

Ὥπερ τὼς Θύννως σκοπιάζεται Ὄλπις ὁ γριπεύς *

* " (I will cast off my coat of skins and into yonder waves I will spring,) where the fisher Olpis watches for the Tunny-shoals." (*Andrew Lang's Translation.*)

More than two thousand years after the time when Olpis was watching, the Rev. J. G. Wood writes of the Tunny, " This magnificent, and most important fish, does not visit our shores in sufficient numbers to be of any commercial value ; but on the shores of the Mediterranean, where it is found in very great abundance, it forms one of the chief sources of wealth to the sea-side population.

" In May and June the Tunnies move in vast shoals along the shores, seeking for suitable spots wherein to deposit their spawn. As soon as they are seen on the move, notice is given by a sentinel, who is constantly watching from some lofty eminence, and the whole population is at once astir, preparing nets for the capture, and salt and tubs for the curing of the expected fish."

There is a perpetual struggle going on between the animals and plants among these hills. The land is unenclosed, and the goats and sheep search everywhere for food. Every blade of grass and every herb that is green and sweet is devoured greedily by the half-starved animals. Only those plants which are very rank or poisonous escape. Hence the fœtid hellebore is found growing with impunity on every hillside and in every valley, for its flavour resembles caustic. The euphorbias, for a similar reason, are not molested, and they number no less than twenty-five species around Mentone.

The Mediterranean quassia (*Cneorum tricoccon*) and the square-stemmed Corriaria, representatives of families not found in Britain, are also protected by their unpleasant properties. They appear all along the Corniche road, and it seems strange that, during the ages they have flourished here, they have not varied as the spurges have, but are confined each to a single genus and a single species.

Until Mr. Andrew Lang showed me a translation of Theocritus which he had lately made, I was under the impression that the goats would not eat the rank leaves of the pistacia bushes (*P. terebinthus*); but, as the ancient Greek author mentions that they nibble them, I watched a flock, and soon found myself corrected by an authority who lived 2000 years ago.

We were not sorry when we reached San Remo, nestling among olive gardens and terraces of orange, lemon, and carob trees. The peaches, almonds, and pears, growing side by side with the Oriental loquats, were in flower, and all round appeared spring-like and beautiful.

On passing through the town towards the hotel where we proposed to pass the night, the sound of many horses' hoofs fell upon our ears, and presently a gay troop of cavaliers came quickly by. The men had broad-brimmed hats adorned with ostrich feathers on their heads, and blue silk cloaks flying in the wind behind, exposed beneath red and purple jackets slashed with gold. Upon their legs they wore blue tights, and jack boots armed with spurs. Each held in his hand a naked sword, and appeared like Agathos, or some

R

good knight one reads about, but never sees. The vision while it lasted was delightful, and was, so we subsequently learnt, connected with a masked ball, to be held in the theatre that night. After parading through the town, the troop came back, and, much to my satisfaction, dismounted close to where we stood. I went up to one of them to see if he was really flesh and blood and not a vision, when suddenly he reeled against the wall, clutched at the bricks to find support, at the same time giving me a vacant stare. I looked no more; for, whatever may have been the condition of his comrades, now turning into a low-roofed tavern, this man was clearly drunk. Truly, I thought, here in Italy as in England, wine is not only used to give a man a cheerful countenance. Nor was this opinion dispelled later by the sounds of revelry, borne on the night air through my open window at the hotel, from the distant low-roofed tavern.

Next morning, before starting for our walk of thirty miles to Alassio, we went to the railway station in order to send on our own luggage, and we were met by a ragged-looking fellow, whom we thought had come to beg; but he took us into the office, wrote out receipts, and did the honours of the place. In fact, as my companion, who has been in Australia, remarked, he was evidently "head boss" there. He presided over a bookstall also, where the only publication for sale was a penny paper, illustrated with a full-page engraving of a horse, labelled "*Afganistan,*" kicking its heels into the air, whilst its rider was sprawling in the dust below. Underneath was the legend, "*John Bull, l'uomo che voleva scendere di sella.*"

Directly we were fairly on our way we had the pleasure of seeing several plants which we had not seen wild before. High up among the crevices of the rocks were mauve-coloured stocks, beautifully conspicuous against a background of yellow stone. Near them were wild cabbages in flower clinging to the precipice, and causing us to wonder how the seed could possibly have got there, and how the roots found sufficient nourishment to support their numerous yellow flowers. Lower down we saw the caper, which had not yet come into flower. I recognised it at once from its resemblance to a cousin which is plentiful in Indian hedgerows. The flowers of both species are large and very beautiful, although the scientific names given them by botanists—"*spinosa*" and "*horrida*"—are not inviting. My friend, Mr. G. Joad, who is very well acquainted with the plants of the Riviera, tells me the European caper is most difficult to grow under glass in England, and that even at Kew its

THE CAMBERWELL BEAUTY.

cultivation hitherto has not been attended with success. But of all the flowers which the Riviera bears, none are more conspicuous and beautiful than the rock roses (*Cistus albidus and C. salvifolius*), which in many places cover the mountain side. It is said that Linnæus, on first seeing the gorse in bloom, knelt down and thanked God for creating such beautiful flowers; and visitors to Mentone need not be ashamed to follow the example of the illustrious Swede when they see the rock roses of the Mediterranean shores. The

R2

flowers are at their best in April, and then many swallow-tailed butterflies hover over them, whilst here and there may be seen the Camberwell Beauty, which is hunted to the death by English collectors.

A few days before we left Mentone for Genoa, I went with a young lepidopterist butterfly-hunting among the hills where I had

THE SWALLOW-TAIL BUTTERFLY.

seen the first Swallow-tails of the season. Upon the road my companion was in an extraordinary state of excitement, and spoke of our chance of success as though the fate of nations depended on our exertions; and when, after an exciting chase, a swallow-tail was caught in his net, he almost went wild with joy. He laughed

and shouted, and rolled upon the ground, starting up again and
again to see that the insect was really there, and that he was not
dreaming he had caught it.   Alas! I thought, if this youth lives as
many years as I have, how many moments will be as happy as
these passed in the capture and death of a poor butterfly?   Even
before we returned home much of the interest of the chase had
passed away, and

> " Our prize, so fiercely sought,
>   Had lost its charm in being caught."

After passing the small town of Port Maurice, we halted in a shady
grove of pines for luncheon, and here at our leisure we could
appreciate the scenery around.   The sky was bright and clear, like
the most beautiful English Summer day.   In a dell beneath our feet
thousands of bees and butterflies were hovering around the heath
flowers and the flowers of many other plants, the most conspicuous
being that representative of an order not found in England, the
button senna (*Globularia alyssum*), the emerald bush spurge (*Euphor-
bia dendroides*), wild rosemary, the prickly pea (*Calycotome spinosa*),
the red valarian, just coming into flower, with here and there,
beneath the pines, primroses and blue hepaticas.   The ground and
air was quite alive with forms representing nearly every division of
the animal kingdom—gold-crests clinging to the branches of the
pines, lizards on the rocks above us, thousands of insects and other
creeping things in the grass below our feet.   We collected in a heap
all the specimens we could find within a radius of six feet from where
we sat, and on counting them up we found forty-two shells of the
spiral land snail (*Cyclostoma elegans*), three shells of the glass snail
(*Helix operta*), one longhorn moth of the genus Adela, a large black
beetle (*Blaps*), a centipede, a locust, an egg case of the praying
mantis, numerous seeds of a juniper bush, and hundreds of com-
pass-like leaves of the Aleppo pine.   Under the pine trees we saw
many spider orchids, which, so rare in England, are common all
along the Riviera ; and associated with them we found the beautiful

yellow orchis (*Ophrys lutea*), and the large wood orchis (*O. longi-bracteatum*). Several other orchids had appeared above the ground, but, not having yet come into flower, we could not ascertain to what species they belonged.

But of all the specimens of natural history found near the Corniche road, the trapdoor spiders are the most famous. They abound in every shady bank, and their curious nests, with a hinged door above, are sought for by every traveller who comes that way. Their history has been partly written, but much remains unknown regarding their habits and domestic economy, and their reason for making doors to their houses, unlike the other members of their tribe. Although apparently a sluggish race, they have spread to every quarter of the globe, and have representatives in Africa, California, Jamaica, Australia, and India.

We had now come thirty-four miles, and the sea had been upon our right below us all the way. On the left were precipices and mountains, with here and there peeps of snow, which crowned the distant Alps. At six o'clock we reached Alassio, as the gong of our hotel was calling travellers to the *table d'hôte*.

After dinner we visited a. *café chantant*, in order to observe how the Italians amused themselves by night. There were about fifty well-dressed people in the room, listening to a comic singer who was illustrating, in song, the proverb " that the course of true love never did run smooth." A pert little damsel was running about, distributing coffee or bock-beer, and cigars to those who smoked. Next to us there sat a mollusc-looking little man, a member of the race "whose heads do grow beneath their shoulders," and whom, with the anthropophagi, Desdemona loved to hear about. He called for beer, and when the damsel brought it, claiming the privilege of an old acquaintance, he squeezed her hand. He then demanded a cigar, and squeezed her hand again. He drank a little of the beer, lit his cigar, and then fell fast asleep, heedless of the music and noise around, and he slumbered till we left. Truly my companion

THE TRAPDOOR SPIDER.

remarked, " Here we see that style of life beloved by thè Italians, and known as *dolce far niente.*"

Next morning again the sun rose in a cloudless sky, and as the basket which I carried the previous day would not hold all the specimens which I had collected for my museum by the way, I bought another of extra size ; leaving the impression, so my com-

GREEN TREE-FROG.

panion declared, that I was carrying weight and walking for a wager, recalling the lines in " Johnny Gilpin,"

" He carries weight, he rides a race,
'Tis for a thousand pounds."

Our road led through terraces of palms and olives, oranges, lemons, vines and carob-bean trees, wherever cultivation was practicable ; and where nature was left unmolested, junipers, Spanish broom, cistus, privet, climbing asparagus, pistacia bushes, evergreen oaks and pines were mingled together, engaged in a Darwinian struggle for existence. Peas and beans are in full bloom, and in one garden some satirical person had put up a scarecrow, in a land where there are no birds to frighten.

But if there are no birds to sing among the branches of the trees, their places are fully occupied by the green frogs, which all day long lie concealed among the friendly-coloured leaves, and only make their presence known when twilight succeeds the day; then the chorus begins, and through the length and breadth of the Riviera a fearful croaking prevails, and lasts throughout the night. Thousands occupy the tanks with which the country abounds, and " fiends in shape of boys " may be seen catching these helpless reptiles and stuffing them into their trouser pockets, either for future amusement or for sale.

Soon after noon we reached Cape Noli, the most beautiful part of the Corniche road. A precipice on our left rose nine hundred and fifty feet straight out of·the sea, and on its summit many a fierce struggle is said to have taken place in days gone by between the inhabitants of these shores and the Algerine pirates ; the vanquished party, or at least those not required for slaves, being flung over the precipice into the sea below. Here we saw for the first time the beautiful red-winged creeper (*Tichodroma muraria*) searching for insects in a small dell among the rocks, where a cascade comes tumbling down the mountain side. It probably had a nest close by, and whilst I was trying to find it my companion made a sketch of the scene around, although his most brilliant colours paled before those of nature, for the rocks reflected indigo, purple, and Naples yellow, with mauve-coloured stocks scattered here and there in company with emerald-coloured spurges. The sky above was cobalt blue, whilst the sea reflected sparkling ultramarine below. Nor did the beauty of the landscape suffer when an express train issued from a tunnel in the rock, sending up a cloud of pure white smoke, which in the still air floated slowly across the precipice and vanished out at sea.

Six hundred feet above us, a pair of Alpine swifts were darting to and fro, selecting a convenient place, secure and dry, in which to build their nest. Their white throats were distinctly visible as we stood below, and we wondered if they appreciated the scenery around, or whether it passed unnoticed. We also wondered what they thought of us from their Agapemone up there. Did they envy us, the lords of creation; or, as they could only see the crowns of our hats, did they rank us as black wingless beetles moving tediously along? This wonderfully beautiful spot appears almost deserted. We saw no signs of anyone along the road, and on the shore below a solitary angler was fishing from the rocks. Truly, I thought, as I watched this man, your lines are cast in pleasant places; but probably he also cared far less for the beauty of the place than its ability to supply him with his daily food.

There are several large caves close by, which were used by men in former days, when house-building was unknown. We climbed up with difficulty into one of them, which was nearly filled by a tremendous rock, fallen from the roof above, and almost hidden by masses of maidenhair ferns. There was another cave a hundred feet above us, inaccessible from below; but, as there is a great hole admitting daylight through the roof, it could probably be entered with the aid of a rope ladder from above. Those who study man's early history would doubtless find many of his relics there. The only present tenant we could see was a blackstart (*Ruticilla tithys*), which had left its pure white eggs, to watch us with jealous eyes so long as we remained in sight.

All along our route the rocks have been laid bare by the workmen who made the road, and the geologist may study the various formations at his leisure. Limestone predominates, and when burnt in furnaces it produces the purest lime known to builders. The water trickling through it has also cemented together vast beds of pebbles, which in ages past formed the shores of primeval seas, kept in constant agitation by the waves and which, so we are told, were trodden by strange forms—lizards, of which the crocodiles of Egypt and India are the puny descendants, by mammoths, and perhaps by man, armed with clubs and weapons tipped with flint, to battle with the beasts around. These pebbly shores in time were covered over by many thousand feet of earth and rock, and have remained buried in the ground for ages. Here and there, however, along the Corniche road they crop out, and in some places large blocks of the conglomerate, or pudding stone, have fallen into the sea. Like Rip van Winkle, the pebbles have started into life again, and, after so many ages of repose, they may be seen rolled to and fro again by the restless sea. Whilst they have been lying underground many changes have taken place overhead ; not only

" The Roman Empire has begun and ended,"

but the animal and vegetable kingdoms, if geologists are right, have almost entirely changed.

Near Savona we found a bed of coarse asbestos or actinolite undistinguishable from specimens which I have from my district in Bengal, and we passed many beds of gritless gault, which would probably repay exportation to England for the manufacture of Portland cement.

Soon after noon we stopped for luncheon at a small roadside inn. A man who was breaking stones by the roadside was singing " *Vien qua, Dorina bella*," and white and red camellias were growing near the door. Peasants basking in the sun were drinking purple wine, and our host congratulated us on our well-timed arrival,; for, as he and his family were on the point of sitting down to dinner, he proposed that we should satisfy our hunger first. We needed no second bidding to the feast, and followed our entertainer to his sleeping chamber, where he gave us hot water to wash our hands, telling us a long story—very little of which we understood—about some honour he had received from Garibaldi. The room to which he led us was almost destitute of furniture. In one corner was a bed, and on the floor close by a cartload of olives lay heaped together; whilst several hundredweight of potatoes were stored about the room. There were many pictures of saints upon the walls, and clay images put wherever they could stand, reminding us of a Bengali's house in India. But, whatever deficiency there may have been in the furniture of the inn, we found no cause to complain of the repast which followed; nor was the reckoning high, being the equivalent of half-a-crown for both of us, including a bottle of what we thought very excellent wine.

Among the plants which we noticed by the way was the wig tree (*Rhus cotinus*), well known in English shrubberies. Its hairy, flowering branches are very conspicuous among the surrounding green foliage, and no one could pass it unnoticed. The daphnes and privets of English gardens are also seen here in great abundance; and in a sandy glen we found the curious prickly bean-caper (*Tribulus terrestris*), which comes very near a common Indian weed whose prickles even elephants are said to dread. By the time we reached Savona the sun had set, and our basket was full of plants, many of which would be marked as prizes by English botanists.

Our walk hitherto had been so pleasant, that with some feelings of regret we left Savona next morning, with the thought that our journey would come to an end that night. The flowers were daily becoming more abundant and conspicuous, and butterflies and insects of every kind and hue were starting into life. But the sun which sustained them was getting very hot, and reminded us of India and Australia. On reaching Voltri we were not sorry to find a *Diligence* was waiting to carry us over the last eight miles of the road, which runs through the outskirts of Genoa, and which is walled on both sides by houses. The outside places were all taken when we arrived, but the two men sitting on the box were persuaded to travel like gentlefolk inside, and give up their plebeian seats to us who wished to see as much of the country as we could, and then we rattled merrily along. Our coachman reminded us of the elder

CPSIA information can be obtained at www.ICGtesting.com
Printed in the USA
BVOW04s1047010615

402667BV00010B/106/P